MELISSA REEVES is a Melbourne playwright. Her plays include *In Cahoots*, *Sweetown* (winner of the 1993 Jill Blewitt Memorial Playwright's Award), *Great Day*, *The Emperor's New Clothes*, *Storming Heaven*, *Road Movie* and *Salt Creek Murders* (winner of the 2001 Wal Cherry Award). She has co-written a number of plays including *The Girl I Love* and *Never Let Me Go* (both with Margaret Mills, Maude Davey and Nicki Redlich); *Magpie* (with Richard Frankland); and *Who's Afraid of the Working Class?* (winner of the 1999 Queensland Premier's Literary Award for Best Drama, two AWGIEs and the 1999 Jill Blewitt Playwright's Award) and *Fever* (both with Andrew Bovell, Patricia Cornelius, Christos Tsiolkas and composer Irine Vela).

Tom Long as Martin and Anna Lise Phillips as Annette in the 2004 Company B production. (Photo: Heidrun Löhr)

THE
SPOOK

MELISSA REEVES

Currency Press, Sydney

CURRENCY PLAYS

First published in 2005
by Currency Press Pty Ltd,
PO Box 2287, Strawberry Hills, NSW, 2012, Australia
enquiries@currency.com.au
www.currency.com.au

NATIONAL LIBRARY OF AUSTRALIA CIP DATA

Reeves, Melissa.
    The spook.
    ISBN 0 86819 768 8.
    I. Title.
    (Series: Currency plays).
  A822.3

Australian Government

Australia Council
for the Arts

Publication of this title was assisted
by the Commonwealth Government
through the Australia Council, its arts
funding and advisory body.

Set by Dean Nottle
Cover design by Kate Florance, Currency Press
Front cover shows Tom Long as Martin in the 2004 Company B production.
Back cover shows Tom Long as Martin and Steve Le Marquand as Alex in
the 2004 Company B production. Photos: Heidrun Löhr

Currency Press acknowledges the Traditional Owners of the Country on which we
live and work. We pay our respects to all Aboriginal and Torres Strait Islander
Elders, past and present.

Contents

Introduction

Stuart Macintyre

'... it's like they've been brainwashed or something... I felt like I wasn't in Bendigo. I don't know where I was... but it was a right little nest of reds on Saturday night.' So Martin Porter records his first impression of a social gathering of communists. Martin, a restless, impressionable nineteen-year-old who works in the railways, is the Spook of Melissa Reeves' historical drama of surveillance, infiltration and betrayal.

The setting is the provincial city of Bendigo—formerly a mining centre, now the regional hub for central Victoria with a mixture of food processing, manufacturing and transport industries in which the Communist Party has a tenuous foothold. The play opens in 1965 and extends over several years. The Communist Party is in decline. The Cold War has exposed it to unrelenting hostility; two decades of economic growth have undermined its message of capitalist crisis; membership has fallen back from 20,000 in the 1940s, 10,000 in the 1950s, to 5,000 by this time.

The Bendigo adherents who Martin encounters are nearly all blow-ins. There is Frank Nash, a veteran activist and the Branch Secretary, who has come from New South Wales, and his partner Phyllis Platten, a school-teacher. There is Mick Leavis, a bearded former seamen, and Jean Bennett, a librarian, who drinks to excess. There are George and Elena Tassakis, political refugees who run a fish-and-chip shop, along with their Greek relatives. The comrades bring an exotic touch to the provincial setting with their wine, dancing and bohemian ways, but their political activity is a dull, unrewarding routine. The branch sells copies of the national newspaper, *Tribune*, around the principal worksites, with little enthusiasm (for, as Jean remarks, a lead article on the inner-city housing shortage has little relevance in Bendigo). It publicises the peace movement and the efforts of other communist parties to conduct movements of national liberation, it holds Russian film evenings and celebrates the achievements of the communist world. These are surrogate forms of political activity, compensating for the lack of local success.

The earlier zeal of the Australian communist movement is spent and the breach between the Soviet Union and the People's Republic of China has already created a schism here. The pro-Chinese faction has recently formed its own breakaway Communist Party of Australia (Marxist-Leninist) and to the ire of Frank Nash, Sam Arnold, 'a nasty ultra-leftist with a foul mouth', is propagating the Chinese line against the 'revisionism' of the Communist Party of Australia. The Party's own criticism of the Soviet Union's invasion of Czechoslovakia in 1968 will bring a further split and compound the divisions in the South Bendigo branch. Theirs is a tired, self-enclosed round of activity and in the absence of more rewarding endeavour, the comrades have turned to purging the backsliders and criticising each other's shortcomings.

It seems bizarre that Australian security should bother with the demoralised 'little nest of reds' in Bendigo. Yet Alex, the local operative of the Australian Security and Intelligence Organisation, surpasses any of the local communists in his zealotry. He has extensive files on their past activity and recruits Martin to obtain additional information. He is quite prepared to invent allegations and plant false documents, for he is in the grip of an obsession that is impervious to reality. In his cups, he tells Martin how he has learned from the head of American counter-intelligence that all the apparent signs of communist disunity—the Hungarian rebellion of 1956, the Czech one of 1968, even the Sino-Soviet split—were all just pretences to divert the West.

With the collapse of communism and the opening of the archives, we now know more of the anti-communist operations of ASIO. During the 1960s it maintained about two hundred agents in anti-communist activity, following Communist Party members, intercepting communications, tapping phones, bugging meeting places, blacklisting members from employment and running spoiling operations. Of all these forms of interference, the use of the spy was perhaps the most debilitating. The Communist Party responded to surveillance with its own security measures, and maintained a strict discipline to withstand repression; but if you could not trust your own comrades then you were left chasing phantoms—hence the common designation of such infiltrators as 'spooks'.

We also know that a nineteen-year-old hospital orderly was recruited by ASIO in Bendigo in 1963. A respected local footballer and member of the Citizens' Military Force, he agreed out of patriotism to become a communist. The Bendigo branch he joined was very small, consisting mainly of elderly people who met in private homes and talked about the workers' cause, but he duly threw himself into service and organised anti-Vietnam demonstrations. 'It was a very lonely time', he has recalled, and he lost most of his friends as well as his marriage, until after two decades ASIO had no further use for him. Following a personal crisis, he told his story to the press in 1991.

From this fragmentary instance of political intrigue Melissa Reeves constructs her play. She gives us Alex as the spymaster. With his dark glasses and other conspiratorial trappings, Alex is as alien to Bendigo as any of the communist characters. He preys on the locals, seeking his own recruits at the local football and inducting them into a world of fantasy. He wants the 'dirt' on Bendigo's communists, their resentments, rivalries, problems with alcohol and money, anything to do with prostitutes, adultery and perversion. And he talks dirty: 'it's a mean cunt of a job, but by God, it's so fucking necessary it's frightening'. The full extent of Alex's ruthlessness will emerge, but he is a constant shadowy presence throughout the drama.

Martin, who serves as his spook, is a more fully realised character. We encounter Martin first in his bedroom, tape-recording a first report on the little nest of reds he is infiltrating. The door is locked, which puzzles his solicitous mother, Trixie, for she is a widow and Martin is her only child. She thinks he might have his girlfriend Annette with him, and his explanation that he is studying for an evening class in history only adds to her unease. This is not the local history of 'gold rushes and things', as Trixie suggests—a suggestion that Martin brushes aside as irrelevant to the imminent threat of nuclear war—it is Marxist history.

We then observe another aspect of Martin's ardour as he sits with his mother and girlfriend watching the popular television quiz program of the period, *Pick-a-Box*. The contestant has chosen to answer questions about the Soviet Union and Martin cannot resist displaying his exhaustive knowledge of its revolutionary history and institutions. Nor is Trixie assuaged by the explanation that he learned this information from that impeccably anti-communist source, *Readers Digest*. 'If your father could see you, he'd turn in his grave', she declares. Annette proposes they change the channel and Martin now wants to watch the glamorous espionage series, *The Man from UNCLE*.

Martin is drawn to the allure of deception. The payment that Alex offers him, three shillings a week, is derisory, but he is intrigued by the tradecraft of political espionage — the drop-point in the park for passing on his intelligence, the half-drawn blind to notify his controller, the arrangements for clandestine meetings. Alex beguiles him with an explanation of how some agents work in deep cover for years with a fake identity, fake papers, fake family history, living a wholly invented life. And a fake wife, Martin suggests.

But Martin is not to be in deep cover, he has to transform himself in full view of those closest to him. Hence his announcement to Annette that he will leave the Citizens' Military Force and grow sideburns is accompanied immediately by a proposal of marriage and the announcement that he is to be a spy. Like Martin, Annette is excited by the transformation but deception proves more difficult than either of them realise. Martin is made physically ill by his acceptance into the Communist Party branch. He is alarmed when Annette seeks to follow him into the Communist Party, more alarmed when she declares to the Bendigo communists her admiration of the British spy Kim Philby, who kept his deception from his wife. 'I think I'm better at it than you are', she tells Martin, and taunts him with his lack of assurance.

The deception of Martin's mother is equally painful. Trixie appeals to Annette not to proceed with the marriage, to talk with the local Catholic priest, to wait and if necessary even to live in sin rather than persist with this godless union. She cannot understand what has happened to her son: '… he was a lovely boy, Martin, he was a lovely patriotic boy with short hair and now look at him'. Trixie is excluded from Martin's new life and responds with angry jibes, to the mounting distress of Annette, who wants Martin to confide in her. By the time he is ready to do so, it is too late: his marriage has broken down and his mother has suffered a stroke. He has betrayed those closest to him.

His life as a spook requires further betrayals. Martin forms a friendship with Elli Tassakis and her husband George. George is a loyalist, Elli increasingly impatient with the dead hand of communist orthodoxy. Here Melissa Reeves draws on the convulsions within the Communist Party of Australia and makes direct reference to the leaders, Laurie Aarons and Bernie Taft, who sought a way out of the impasse. Their open criticism of the Soviet Union's repression of Czechoslovakia was followed by a further liberalisation of the Australian party. Frank Nash won't have a bar of the reforms of these 'bloody Jewish intellectuals'; Elli Tassakis leads the Bendigo branch in welcoming them. The brutal crushing of the 'Prague Spring' has crystallised Elli's weariness with the sterile conformity of a movement that has betrayed its ideals. 'There's something dead about it', she declares, 'It's dull and vicious, defending itself all the time, like a siege mentality'.

In this mood of disillusionment she bickers with George, and tells Martin how her husband was a marked man in Greece, a member of a leading Communist family and marked for elimination by the anti-communist regime installed after the civil war in that country. Hence he had adopted his cousin's name, Tassakis, to gain entry to Australia. This is the secret that Martin passes on to his controller, and leads inexorably to the deportation of both George and Elli.

It is both a political and a personal betrayal—Martin makes clumsy advances to Elli—and completes his disillusionment. Hitherto Martin has followed instructions, supporting Frank Nash's hard line against the liberals, but Elli now reveals that Frank has always suspected him of being a spook. His capacity to dissemble is exhausted. He tries to ring ASIO but cannot. He appeals for support to Annette but it is too late. He attempts to explain to his mother but she cannot understand him. He is left in the end with Alex, his controller, who he knows has lied to him and used him, and is likely to do so again.

The Spook is a political drama of tight precision. The circles of deceit are all completed, and they enclose all the characters within them. The idealists, the cynics and the apolitical are all caught up in a web of manipulation and distortion. The play is marked by a close knowledge of its subject, its time and place. Some might see it as a statement of disillusion with radical politics, but this is surely to mistake the purpose.

It is a tragedy of innocence and temptation, but it is also a reminder of the distorting prism of surveillance. How might a similar dramatisation of security operations illuminate today's War on Terror?

Stuart Macintyre is the Ernest Scott Professor of History at the University of Melbourne and has written extensively about the left in Britain and Australia. In 1998 he published The Reds, *a history of Australian communism from its origins until 1942; he is currently working on the sequel.*

Playwright's Note

Melissa Reeves

In 1991 I was very struck by an article in the paper, in which Phil Geri revealed to the world that he had spent 22 years working for ASIO as an undercover agent, a 'sparrow' in a communist party branch in Bendigo. This was the impetus for *The Spook*. While noting that my play is a fictional version of such a story, I'd like to thank Phil Geri for sharing his story with me. I'd also like to thank the people who told me the companion stories of the communists, and their courageous and confusing struggles through the turmoil of the fifties and sixties: Kay Alexiou, Peg Cregan, Bernice Morris, Olga Silver and Mick Tsounis. I would also like to thank the Literature Board of the Australia Council, the Australian National Playwrights' Conference, and Neil Armfield and Company B Belvoir.

Melbourne
October 2005

The Spook was first produced by Company B at the Belvoir St Theatre, Sydney, on 4 November 2004 with the following cast:

ELLI / DOLLY DYER	Eugenia Fragos
FRANK / AGENT 2	Russell Kiefel
MARTIN	Tom Long
ALEX / FANTASY COMMUNIST	Steve Le Marquand
ANNETTE / JEAN / POLICEWOMAN	Anna Lise Phillips
GEORGE / FOOTBALLER	George Spartels
TRIXIE / PHYLLIS	Kerry Walker

Director, Neil Armfield
Set Design, Ralph Myers
Lighting Design, Damien Cooper
Composer, Alan John
Sound Design, Steve Francis
Costume Design, Jennie Tate

CHARACTERS

MARTIN
TRIXIE
ANNETTE
ALEX
FRANK
PHYLLIS
JEAN
ELLI
GEORGE
POLICEWOMAN
VINCENT
FOOTBALLER

For a cast of seven, doubling is suggested as follows:

TRIXIE / PHYLLIS
ANNETTE / JEAN / POLICEWOMAN
GEORGE / FOOTBALLER
FRANK / VINCENT

ACT ONE: 1965

SCENE ONE

Music, laughter and late night conversation can be heard from behind a dimly-lit closed door. The door opens and light floods out. There is a glimpse of people dancing, a flash of a green dress. A beautiful Greek woman in her forties emerges and closes the door. She walks offstage and after a few moments comes back with a couple of bottles of beer. She glances towards the audience as if to reassure herself of something. She opens the door. Warmth and noise flood out. It is a tantalising room. She walks in to a surge of welcome and shuts the door.

◆ ◆ ◆ ◆ ◆

SCENE TWO

MARTIN *is sitting in his bedroom. He is nineteen years old. He has a brand new tape recorder on the desk in front of him, with a tiny microphone set up on a stand. He presses record.*

MARTIN: Testing. Testing. This is... Iago.

He turns off the record button, rewinds and plays it back.

[*Voice on tape*] Testing. Testing. This is... Iago.

He presses stop. He pauses. He presses record.

Last night, the fourteenth of October, I attended a party at nineteen Brighton Avenue, East Bendigo, the home of Elena and George Tassakis. They appear to be Greek.

He pauses.

I arrived at the party at nineteen hundred hours. At that stage of the evening there were four people present. George Tassakis, Elena Tassakis, Chris Tassakis and Cally Tassakis. Wine was served. George Tassakis said he'd made it himself. He showed me a barrel in the shed. It was full of wine. He said he'd been making his own wine for seven years and this was the best yet. Chris Tassakis and Cally Tassakis were given wine to drink. They are eight and twelve years old.

He presses pause. He looks at his notes. He presses record.

Altogether twenty-seven people attended the party at Brighton Avenue. I succeeded in learning eleven names. George Tassakis. He's about fifty years old, short, with a round face, going bald. He has a fish-and-chip shop. Elena Tassakis, that's his wife, quite pretty...

He rewinds and replays to find the spot and wipes 'quite pretty'.

She's younger than her husband, with a slight build. Long black hair. She stayed in the kitchen for most of the night, until the dancing began. Chris Tassakis, their young son. Cally Tassakis, their daughter. Very precocious. She handed out little slogans reading—'Stop the Imperialist War'—and asked me if I was a communist. I told her you don't ask people questions like that. She said, in this house you do. In this house you nail your colours to the mast. By this she presumably meant the huge Soviet flag hanging on the chimney. She said, come into my bedroom and play cards with me. I said, why in your bedroom? She said, you'll understand if I tell you what sort of cards I want to play. I said, what sort of cards do you want to play? She said, strip poker. I said, where did you learn to play strip poker? She said, at the Eureka Youth Club. That's the communist youth club they've got here, like a sort of commie girl guides. I said, what else do you do at the Eureka Youth Club? She said they do Russian peasant dancing.

He consults his notes.

Jean Bennett, a lady about thirty years old, thin with mousy brown hair. She lives in Leichhardt Street, Bendigo, works in the library. Drank to excess. Raylene Bennett, her sister, a cosmetician. She left the party early, said she'd rather be at home listening to the radio. She tried to make her sister go with her but her sister wouldn't go. They fought quite loudly at the gate.

He consults his notes.

Manni Dimitriades, something like that. I'm reasonably sure he was a cousin to Georges Tassakis. Been in Australia three years. Got a very thick accent. Frank Nash, about fifty, bushy hair, strong well-built sort of bloke. I've seen him round town. He works at the Railway Transit office in Currie Street. Wouldn't have picked him for a commie in a million years. And Phyllis, dunno her last name, missed it. Arrived with Frank Nash. They're definitely not married to each other, but they were... intimate, you know. She has reddish brown hair and a high-pitched laugh, like a horse, and she wore this low-cut green satin dress and high heels. She spent most of the night in the kitchen with Elena Tassakis. They both came out when the dancing began. She was mad with Frank Nash for not dancing with her, so later she danced on her own and made a spectacle of herself.

He switches off the record button. He takes out a packet of cigarettes he has hidden under the table. He is nervous and excited. He lights a cigarette, smokes half of it, blowing the smoke out the window. He butts it out and goes back to the tape recorder, consults his notes and presses record.

There's two more I got names for. Lance Whitney, middle-aged bloke, missing two fingers on his right hand... and Mick Leavis, the guy that sold me the *Tribune* in the pub. A big bloke with a beard, says he went to Russia when he was twenty-five as a merchant seaman, says it was like he saw a vision of heaven and he's been a communist ever since... Oh and there was Paul something or other, a dentist, left pretty early... I missed the rest. I didn't wanna write anything down, even in the dunny, you know, like you said, but anyway... What else...?

After supper everyone gathered in the backyard. George Tassakis introduced Frank Nash as the reddest red in Australia. Frank Nash made a speech thanking Elena and George and talked about the Soviet Union and China and said China was making it very difficult for the Soviets to send their weapons into North Vietnam. He said things were in a sorry state if China could forbid the Soviets to use their air-space and tell them to catch the train. He said that it's very damaging for international communism, and that someone called Sam Arnold had wanted to show his Chinese slides at this very get-together, but that Lance had told him to go and book the Town Hall and see how many turned up. Everyone laughed. Then he said, raise your glasses to the workers of the world and the Communist Party of the Soviet Union, and everybody cheered. Incredible, you know, the neighbours could hear all this stuff. Then people did these little performances. Mick Leavis did a poem, something about a man dying down a mine, and the cousin, Dimitriades, did a Greek dance to a record on the record-player that they brought out into the garden, he was pretty good, he was a bit of a hit with the ladies, and then Lance Whitney, the guy with the two fingers missing, he bloody well played the banjo while the lady that works in the library, Jean, did a hula dance in a grass skirt. Most people started leaving after that. There was a bit more singing and dancing and stuff, and they passed a hat around collecting money for a man in prison in Greece, someone called Glazzo. The stayers didn't finish up until o-two-thirty or so in the morning, with the men sitting around in the kitchen talking about the election, bagging Menzies, and the ladies washing the glasses, chiming in with stuff. The women seem just as deep in it as the men, couldn't believe it, the words that came out their mouths, it's like they've been brainwashed or something... I felt like I wasn't in Bendigo. I don't know where I was... but it was a right little nest of reds on Saturday night. After Frank Nash left they played cards for money. I lost seven shillings.

He pauses.

I was wondering if I get that back at all?

TRIXIE: [*offstage*] Martin.

MARTIN *jumps.* TRIXIE *knocks on the door.*

Martin, what are you doing in there?

MARTIN: Nothing, Mum. I'll be out in a minute.

She tries the door.

TRIXIE: [*offstage*] What've you locked yourself in for?

MARTIN: I'm just doing a bit of study, Mum.

TRIXIE: [*offstage*] What are you studying for?

MARTIN: For my evening class.

TRIXIE: [*offstage*] Have you got Annette in there?

MARTIN *is swiftly putting away his tape recorder and hiding his notes.*

MARTIN: No.

TRIXIE: [*offstage*] Annette, are you in there?

There is no response.

What evening class?

MARTIN: I told you last week. I'm taking an evening class.

TRIXIE: [*offstage*] What for?

MARTIN: Just for interest.

TRIXIE: [*offstage*] Let me in.

> MARTIN *opens the door. His mother,* TRIXIE, *stands there in the dim light peering in the door.*

Why are you so excited about studying all of a sudden?

MARTIN: I just want to do this one course.

TRIXIE: What course is it?

MARTIN: History.

TRIXIE: What sort of history is it?

MARTIN: It's just history, Mum.

TRIXIE: What sort of history?

MARTIN: It's just history, all right?

> *Pause.*

TRIXIE: Gold rushes and things. Is that what you're studying?

MARTIN: No that's not what I'm studying. Do you think that's what's important in the world today, Mum? Jesus Christ, Mum… the whole goddamned country could be blown up any goddamned bloody minute and then what would be the bloody point of knowing about stinking gold rushes?! [*Pause.*] I'm sorry.

TRIXIE: That's all right.

> *Pause.*

MARTIN: I'm studying Marx's theory of dialectical materialism.

◆ ◆ ◆ ◆ ◆

SCENE THREE

MARTIN, ANNETTE *and* TRIXIE *are watching TV.*

DOLLY: [*on the TV*] This is Margaret, Bob. Margaret works in Grace Brothers.

BOB: [*on the TV*] How're you feeling, Margaret?

MARGARET: [*on the TV*] Okay.

BOB: [*on the TV*] Heart beating a little?

MARGARET: [*on the TV*] A bit.

ANNETTE: She's having kittens.

TRIXIE: Sshh.

BOB: [*on the TV*] Are you ready to play Pick-a-Box?

MARGARET: [*on the TV*] I think so.

BOB: [*on the TV*] All right, Margaret. Your choices are: Great Rivers, Famous Faces, Twentieth Century, Comparisons, Spelling, The Antarctic, Countries of the World, American Indians, or Man's Best Friend…

ANNETTE: She'll take spelling.

MARGARET: [*on the TV*] Countries of the World please.

ANNETTE: She should have / taken spelling.

BOB: [*on the TV*] Barry, could you enter the soundproof booth and put on your headphones…

TRIXIE: Barry's not the only one who should enter the soundproof booth.

BOB: [*on the TV*] Margaret, you have two minutes. Your time starts now… What do the letters USSR stand for?

MARTIN: The Union of / Soviet Socialist Republics.

MARGARET: [*on the TV*] The United States of Soviet… Republics.

BOB: [*on the TV*] I'm sorry that's incorrect, it's the Union of Soviet Socialist Republics. If I were foolhardy enough to meet you at the Kremlin, where would I be meeting you?

MARTIN: It's the Soviet parliament / building in Moscow.

MARGARET: [*on the TV*] Pass.

BOB: [*on the TV*] It's the seat of Russian government in Moscow. A landmark in the same city, how would I recognise St Basil's?

MARTIN: You'd recognise the coloured onion / domes on the roof.

MARGARET: [*on the TV*] Pass.

BOB: [*on the TV*] You'd know it by it's distinctive multi-coloured onion-shaped domes.

ANNETTE: Jesus.

TRIXIE: Annette!

BOB: [*on the TV*] If I was a *babushka*, what would I be?

MARTIN: An old / lady.

MARGARET: [*on the TV*] A baby.

BOB: [*on the TV*] Wrong, an elderly lady or grandmother. In what year did the Russian Revolution take place and by what other name is it known?

MARGARET: [*on the TV*] Nineteen...

MARTIN: The Bolshevik Revolution and it took place in October, 1917.

MARGARET: [*on the TV*] Pass.

BOB: [*on the TV*] The October or Bolshevik Revolution and it took place in 1917.

> TRIXIE *is becoming bewildered and emotional.*

Alexander Pushkin, Boris Pasternak, and Fyodor Dostoyevsky are famous Russian what?

MARTIN: Writers.

MARGARET: [*on the TV*] Gymnasts.

BOB: Wrong. Writers. The name of the first Russian astronaut to orbit in space was...

MARTIN & MARGARET: [*together*] Yuri Gagarin.

BOB: [*on the TV*] Correct. Complete the name of this famous book that purports to tell the story of the Russian Revolution. *Ten Days that—*

MARGARET: [*on the TV*] Pass.

MARTIN: *Shook the World.*

BOB: [*on the TV*] *Shook the World.* Petrograd, Leningrad and Stalingrad are cities in Communist Russia. What did they used to be called?

MARTIN: Petrograd and Leningrad are the same place—St Petersburg, Stalingrad was known as / Tsaritsyn.

MARGARET: [*on the TV*] Pass.

BOB: [*on the TV*] It's a tricky one, Margaret, Petrograd and Leningrad are the same place and were previously known as St Petersburg. Stalingrad was previously called Tsaritsyn. What is both a colour in the Russian flag and the colloquial term for a communist sympathiser?

MARTIN & MARGARET: [*together*] Red.

BOB: [*on the TV*] Correct and your time's up, Margaret. You have twenty points. Dolly, can you tell Barry he can come out of the booth now... / And we'll be back after a word from our sponsors...

> ANNETTE *and* TRIXIE *are staring at* MARTIN.

MARTIN: What?

ANNETTE: How'd you know all that stuff?

MARTIN: I just knew it.

ANNETTE: I don't remember you being that clever at school.

> MARTIN *doesn't respond.*

You should go on it.

MARTIN: I wasn't that good.

ANNETTE: You got every question. About Russia.

> MARTIN *glances at his mother.*

MARTIN: It's the *Readers Digest*.

ANNETTE: What?

MARTIN: I got it all from the *Readers Digest*. Mum buys it.

TRIXIE: I don't buy it for its articles on communism. [*Pause.*] What do you think you're playing at?

MARTIN: Nothing.

TRIXIE: What are you mucking about with all this for?

MARTIN: I'm not mucking about, Mum.

TRIXIE: If your father could see you, he'd turn in his grave.

> TRIXIE *leaves.* ANNETTE *turns down the TV.*

ANNETTE: What's going on?

MARTIN: Nothing…

ANNETTE: What's she so upset about?

MARTIN: Just… arguments about politics…

ANNETTE: What about politics?

MARTIN: Just about capitalism… and communism, stuff like that… [*Pause.*] A lot of people don't shine at school, you know. A lot of famous people don't. Almost the inverse if anything.

> ANNETTE *doesn't respond.*

Albert Einstein. Churchill. Nobel Prize winners. People like that. You take a look at their school records. I guarantee you. Most of them won't have done very well. Cs, Ds, Es. Marks like that. Fs even… It's not a prerequisite for doing something important in the world.

> *Pause.* BOB DYER *can still be heard on the TV.*

BOB: [*on the TV*] Howdy, customers, and welcome back Barry, / our defending champion, who's about to play Pick-a-Box.

MARTIN: Let's change the channel.

ANNETTE: What do you want to watch?

MARTIN: *The Man from UNCLE.*

◆ ◆ ◆ ◆ ◆

SCENE FOUR

ALEX *is standing in the park. He has on dark glasses.* MARTIN *joins him. He also has on dark glasses.*

ALEX: Your stuff's great.

MARTIN: Yeah?

ALEX: Very high grade. I'm impressed.

MARTIN: Yeah...? That's the sort of thing?

ALEX: Oh, yeah...

MARTIN: That's what you want?

ALEX: Yeah...

> *They are silent for a few moments.*

There's a couple of things.

MARTIN: Yeah.

ALEX: Can you take those glasses off...

> MARTIN *takes off his dark glasses.*

What's this shit with Iago?

MARTIN: It's in Shakespeare.

ALEX: Yeah, I know who he is.

MARTIN: I didn't want to use my real name.

ALEX: You're Q24.

> MARTIN *nods.*

All right?

MARTIN: Right.

ALEX: It's not that I want to spoil your fun but it's too confusing, we've got an Iago.

MARTIN: Oh, right.

ALEX: Yeah.

MARTIN: Wow.

ALEX: Yeah... He's in deep cover, you know what that is?

MARTIN: No.

ALEX: This stuff I tell you, this is classified. This is not for public consumption.

MARTIN: Yeah, I know.

ALEX: This is second-gear stuff.

MARTIN: I understand.

ALEX: Deep cover is where we give someone a totally fabricated identity. He's got a fake name, fake papers, fake family history, the lot, and he lives his life as this person, he marries as this person, he has kids as this person, gets a job… But he does nothing, nothing at all, just lives out this invented life. It might be ten years, fifteen years before we need him. We might never need him.

MARTIN: Never?

ALEX: It's unlikely, but it's possible.

MARTIN: But what if you never need him? Does he die as the fake person?

ALEX: He might.

MARTIN: And the fake wife would put the wrong name on his gravestone.

ALEX: She's not a fake wife. He's fake, she's not fake… Anyway I'd think we'd probably tell him if we thought we weren't going to need him.

MARTIN: And what, he'd get a divorce.

ALEX: You're grabbing the wrong end of the stick, Martin. He likes his wife. He finds someone he likes. If he doesn't find anybody he doesn't get married. The point is he sits and waits.

Tom Long (left) as Martin and Steve Le Marquand as Alex in the 2004 Company B production. (Photo: Heidrun Löhr)

MARTIN: Right.

ALEX: For years at a time, and one day, he'll be reading the *Herald*, like he does every day, and he'll turn to the classifieds, and there'll be a couple of lines that catch his eye.

MARTIN: Like out of Shakespeare.

ALEX: Maybe.

MARTIN: Like out of *Othello* so he knows he has to come in.

ALEX: You're smart, Martin.

MARTIN: Is he going to have to kill someone? Is that what he is? An assassin?

ALEX: No, I don't think so.

MARTIN: And he's really out there. Iago. He's really out there. Waiting.

ALEX: Yeah. Now I want to talk about money.

MARTIN: Okay.

ALEX: Now I know you a bit now and I know how strongly you feel about those commie bastards…

MARTIN *nods.*

… and you probably would have done this stuff for nothing if I'd asked you, but I didn't ask you, 'cause I want you for the long haul, Martin, I want you once the initial thrill has worn off, when it's just hard work, 'cause that's what it is, I'm not going to lie to you, it's a mean cunt of a job, but by God, it's so fucking necessary it's frightening. We could tip either way. If you're not working in security you may as well be masturbating in bed, honestly, that's why we're giving you three shillings, three shillings for each and every week you work for us… Okay?

MARTIN *nods.*

We'll start paying you as soon as you become a member of the Party… Have they asked you to a meeting yet?

MARTIN: No.

ALEX: That's all right. They will.

MARTIN: They ask me to all their social things.

ALEX: No need to be too eager. Slowly slowly catchee monkey. Buy their paper, read their paper. Start making a few noises at work. You're a member of the union?

MARTIN: Nah… Oh, maybe I am.

ALEX: Oh, Jesus, you've got to be in the union.

MARTIN: Do I?

ALEX: Yes. You've gotta wave the red flag, Martin.

MARTIN: What if I get into trouble?

ALEX: Get a name for yourself. And send us more stuff when you've been to your first meeting.

MARTIN: The same method?

ALEX: What did you do last time?

MARTIN: I left it in the elm tree in the park.

ALEX: How was that?

MARTIN: It was good.

ALEX: Let's try the pictures this time.

MARTIN: Okay.

ALEX: You got a blind in your bedroom, a holland blind?

MARTIN: Yep.

ALEX: Okay, the week before the drop, you pull the blind in your bedroom down to halfway, you leave it like that, the following Wednesday—

MARTIN: That's my class in Historical Materialism.

ALEX: Okay, Thursday. You go to the early session—have they got an early session?

MARTIN: Six o'clock.

ALEX: You go to the six o'clock session, whatever's on, you sit in the third row, ten seats in from the left. You—

MARTIN: What if there's someone sitting there?

ALEX: You make sure you get there early. But if there is someone there, sit in the aisle seat, second row, on the left—

MARTIN: The left side of the left aisle?

ALEX: No just the left aisle—

MARTIN: No, but there's three banks of seating, there's the main one in the middle, then there's a skinny one on the left and a skinny one on the right—

ALEX: I got you, okay, the backup is the aisle seat, in the second row, on the inside of the left-side block of seating, the skinny block.

MARTIN: That's not a very good seat.

ALEX: That's the point, Martin, if it's a good seat it's more likely to be sat in. So you just leave your stuff under the seat and someone'll get it, okay, names are the most important, we want every name, every name, not only people at the meeting, but every name that's mentioned. You got that?

MARTIN: Yeah.

ALEX: So once you're in, a good job to get would be something to do with checking people are financial, or looking after the *Tribune* sales, something like that, again, don't leap in too quick, let them take the lead, also pick up any paperwork you see lying around and can filch it without getting spotted, we love that stuff, so that's names, that's paperwork, that's number one, all right…? What do you think number two is?

MARTIN: Politics…

ALEX *shakes his head.*

Protests… Stuff about the Soviet Union…

ALEX: Number two is dirt. That's why I liked your stuff. You've got a feel for the personal detail. I felt like I was at the party. I saw those people you talked about. The slut in the green dress. The wog that can dance. It's lovely, that's lovely stuff. That's what we want. Resentments, rivalries, problems with alcohol, problems with money, anything to do with sex, prostitutes, adultery, perversion. Now that stuff won't necessarily happen at the meetings, you gotta find a way of getting it. Okay?

MARTIN: Okay.

ALEX: Number three is the obvious, the meeting, what is said and who says it, just the facts, don't you go drawing any conclusions, that's our job. Okay, let's leave it at that.

MARTIN: There's just one thing… um…

ALEX: Alex. You are allowed to use my name.

MARTIN: Is that your real name?

ALEX: 'Course it's not my real name. What do you want?

MARTIN: I'm worried about my girlfriend.

ALEX: She's a problem?

MARTIN: No, no… Just all this commie stuff. I don't know how she's going to take it.

ALEX: How long you been going out with her?

MARTIN: About two years.

ALEX: What's she like?

MARTIN: She's nice.

ALEX: She screw around?

MARTIN: No.

ALEX: She take any drugs, she smoke pot?

MARTIN: No, she doesn't do anything like that.

ALEX: Heh, it's all right. I gotta ask these things. Annette, right?

> MARTIN *hesitates a moment.* ALEX *gets out a notebook.*

MARTIN: Yeah…

ALEX: Annette…?

MARTIN: Craigy.

ALEX: How old is she?

MARTIN: Nineteen.

ALEX: Born here?

MARTIN: Yeah.

ALEX: What's her mother's name?

MARTIN: Rosalind.

ALEX: No, her maiden name.

MARTIN: I dunno.

ALEX: What's her address?

MARTIN: Twelve Curnow Street, Bendigo.

> ALEX *puts his notebook away and slaps* MARTIN *on the shoulder.*

ALEX: Well done, Martin.

◆ ◆ ◆ ◆ ◆

SCENE FIVE

MARTIN *and* ANNETTE *are sitting on the couch.*

MARTIN: I've got something to tell you.

ANNETTE: What?

> *Pause.*

MARTIN: I'm leaving the CMF.

ANNETTE: You're what?

MARTIN: The Citizens' Military Force. It's getting in the way of my work.

ANNETTE: At the railway?

> MARTIN *pauses.*

MARTIN: Do you want to get married?

ANNETTE *pauses.*

ANNETTE: Yeah.

MARTIN *gets up and pulls down the blinds.*

MARTIN: Where's Mum?

ANNETTE: She went out.

MARTIN: Did you see her go?

ANNETTE: Yeah.

MARTIN: She went out the door?

ANNETTE *doesn't reply.*

Did you see her go out the front door?

ANNETTE: Yes. Come over here.

MARTIN *looks into another room and checks the hall.*

Martin… I saw her leaving.

MARTIN: Sshh.

ANNETTE: What?

MARTIN: Keep your voice down.

ANNETTE: Why?

MARTIN: You talk too loud.

ANNETTE: What do you mean I talk too loud?

MARTIN: You've got a very loud voice.

ANNETTE: I haven't.

MARTIN: I think you should try talking a bit softer.

ANNETTE: I'm not going to try and talk a bit softer. What's wrong with
  you?

MARTIN: Nothing. [*Pause.*] There's something I've got to tell you.

ANNETTE: What?

MARTIN: Something that will really affect our life together.

ANNETTE: What… is it about your mother?

MARTIN: No.

ANNETTE: What is it?

MARTIN: I'm a spy.

ANNETTE: What?

MARTIN: I'm a spy. For the government.

ANNETTE: What do you mean?

MARTIN: I spy on people.

ANNETTE: Who?

MARTIN: I'm allowed to tell you I'm a spy because we're getting married but I'm not allowed to go into detail about it.

ANNETTE: Do I know them?

MARTIN: Maybe.

ANNETTE: A spy! How long have you been a spy!

MARTIN: Eight months… I haven't started the actual spying yet, I mean I have, but I'm not in position yet.

ANNETTE: You've got to get in position.

MARTIN: Yeah.

ANNETTE: What sort of position?

MARTIN: I've got to gain the trust of the people that I have to spy on.

ANNETTE: Martin.

MARTIN: I know.

ANNETTE: It's incredible.

MARTIN: I know.

ANNETTE: A spy… Do you have to do all that sort of… spy stuff?

MARTIN: What do you mean spy stuff?

ANNETTE: Invisible writing and stuff.

> MARTIN *sits next to her on the couch.*

MARTIN: It's not like in books… or films, you know… James Bond and that… I mean there's some of that stuff… trade craft… that's what it's called, it's not all made up, but… when it's real… when it's real people… it's so frightening…

ANNETTE: Oh, Martin.

> *She moves closer to him. He is incredibly serious and she is finding it quite arousing. They say nothing for a moment.*

MARTIN: I have to grow sideburns.

ANNETTE: Why?

MARTIN: I dunno… to look more… revolutionary.

> ANNETTE *laughs then becomes serious.*

ANNETTE: Touch my breasts.

> *He touches her breasts. They smile at each other.*

How did you get into it?

MARTIN: He just came up to me, at a football game… this bloke, out of the blue, and he said, Martin, and I said, yeah, thinking how does this bloke know my name, and thinking I have to get back to the game, I was playing in the game, you know, I was the forward pocket, it was crazy, and he said, I've been watching you and I like the way you play your football, and I said, yeah, well I better get back to it, and then he said... how much do you love your country, Martin? Imagine just asking someone that... How much do you love your country, Martin? And I said, I dunno... He said he could tell by the way I play football that I loved my country. Sounds stupid, doesn't it?

ANNETTE: He picked you out to be a spy 'cause of how you played football.

MARTIN: Weird, eh.

ANNETTE: Who is he?

MARTIN: Just this bloke...

ANNETTE: You do play really good.

MARTIN: Yeah, I s'pose...

> *She rubs up against him...* MARTIN *responds.*

But do you think that's how they get spies, they go round to all the sports matches, and they recruit all the good players?

ANNETTE: Maybe they want them to be really fit.

MARTIN: Anyway, then he said he wanted to talk to me about something important, something that would change my life, something that had to be kept secret, whatever happened, no one must know about our conversation, I went, oh yeah, well perhaps the best place to talk isn't the middle of a football game where I'm one of the players... and he said, nah, it's the best time, it's the best place, and I laughed, and he said, no one's looking at you, are they... and I looked up, and you know what, Annette?

ANNETTE: What?

MARTIN: He was right. No one was looking at us. The coach, the crowd... No one.

ANNETTE: Wow.

> *They kiss and get more excited.*

MARTIN: You're the only person I can tell.

ANNETTE: Wow.

MARTIN: I can't tell Mum, he said, just you.

ANNETTE: Oh, Martin.

MARTIN: He said if we got married I could tell you.

    Pause.

ANNETTE: We're not married.

MARTIN: Yeah, but you said yes.

ANNETTE: What if I change my mind?

MARTIN: You can't now… you can't change your mind now…

ANNETTE: Can't I?

MARTIN: You said yes… you said you'd marry me.

ANNETTE: Maybe you should have waited a few days, Martin, before you told me.

MARTIN: You seemed certain enough.

ANNETTE: Well, I am certain… but what if I wake up tomorrow and think this is the wrong thing…?

MARTIN: You can't…

ANNETTE: I might.

MARTIN: Oh, Jesus, you agreed to it, we have to get married.

From left: Russell Kiefel, Eugenia Fragos, Steve Le Marquand, George Spartels and Kerry Walker in the 2004 Company B production. (Photo: Heidrun Löhr)

ANNETTE: We don't have to do anything... I might want to live together for a few years first.

MARTIN: Oh no... Annette... that's... no... I told him we were getting married. Properly. We've got to get married. We can't live together. He particularly said married. We have to get married. You said you'd marry me...

Pause.

ANNETTE: Who are you spying on?

Pause.

MARTIN: The Bendigo Communist Party.

ANNETTE: God...

MARTIN *nods.*

MARTIN: I've got to become a member.

ANNETTE: God... the Communist Party. You're going to become a member of the Communist Party... God... Oh, my God.

MARTIN: I know.

ANNETTE: Who are they? Do I know them?

MARTIN: I can't tell you.

ANNETTE: Have you met them or do you just follow them around?

MARTIN: I don't follow anyone around... I'm not that sort of spy.

ANNETTE: So what do you have to do?

MARTIN: I've got to go to their meetings. When they ask me if I'd like to join.

ANNETTE: What do they do at their meetings?

MARTIN: I don't know. I haven't been yet...

◆ ◆ ◆ ◆ ◆

SCENE SIX

Five people run onto the stage. They are dressed in fur caps and coats and boots. They are all smoking. They talk to each other in Russian. They laugh maliciously. One of them pours little shot glasses of vodka. They drink them down. A woman hitches up her skirt and starts doing sexy Cossack dancing. The men join in. They exit, dancing.

◆ ◆ ◆ ◆ ◆

SCENE SEVEN

MARTIN *is alone in his room, trying to make his blind stay at halfway. It wants to be either up or down and won't stay at halfway. He gets increasingly frustrated. The blind comes completely off its hinges. Somehow, he fudges it into position.*

◆ ◆ ◆ ◆ ◆

SCENE EIGHT

FRANK, PHYLLIS, ELLI, GEORGE, JEAN *and* MARTIN *are sitting around a table at Elli's house. It is early in the evening. The mood is a bit dull and slow.*

FRANK: There's a couple of things on the local front… Bert Mangus seems to backing the Unity Ticket…

> *Grunts of mild interest.*

I have to say I'm hesitant about the whole thing, with their track record, but well, if they want to be on the ticket, that's good news as far as we're concerned… Come July, they'll probably turn around and wriggle out of it like they did in '63. But, who knows? Maybe they've realised they backed the wrong horse… They looked pretty bloody foolish after the huge gains we made last year, and there's no doubt they want a bit of reflected glory, well, Bert almost admitted as much to me, and they could do with it, the Labor Party's been on the nose since the miners' strike, so for the moment, they're with us, well, it looks like they're with us… [*pause*] … which means we've got a definite majority as far as the overtime dispute goes, and we're putting the other issues to him… Did he have a word to you…? Right… so the railway fraction will be dealing with that and that's perhaps all we need say about that for the minute… [*pause*] … but I think with those sort of numbers we haven't really got anything to worry about… not in the short term anyway… We'll talk about Peter Digby later on, I take it…

> GEORGE *nods.*

What's next, Phyll?

PHYLLIS: *Tribune.*

Pause. FRANK *rubs his face. Everyone looks down.*

FRANK: I'm afraid the sales of *Tribunes* have continued on their downward trend. I don't need to remind anybody how important it is that we keep selling the paper. It's the lifeblood of the Party. Now apparently there's been no one outside Vicars, or Heinz, or the abattoirs. Jean, that's your beat, isn't it?

JEAN: I thought I was doing Heinz... and I have been.

FRANK: You're not Vicars?

JEAN: No.

FRANK: Who is Vicars?

No one answers.

Well, I'd give Vicars to you, Jean, but you don't seem to be making a very good job of Heinz.

JEAN: I think I missed one morning and one evening... and maybe one other evening...

FRANK: How many papers did you sell last week?

JEAN: Seventeen.

Pause.

FRANK: And how many did you sell for the month?

JEAN: I haven't really added it up yet...

No one says anything as she nervously adds up her figures.

Um... thirty-four... no thirty-five.

FRANK: That's not nearly good enough. Not for the factory round. We should be selling sixty plus... George, can you—?

JEAN: It was the cover.

FRANK *looks at her. She nervously continues.*

It was all about inner-city housing. I don't think people in Bendigo really care if you can't get a house in Collingwood or... Alexandria or wherever...

FRANK: I think you're underestimating the working class, comrade. So who's been selling at the abattoirs? Has anyone been selling at the abattoirs? [*To* JEAN] You've not been selling at the abattoirs?

JEAN: No.

FRANK: Well, why is your name here?

JEAN: I don't know.

ELLI: I think that was a temporary thing, a while back… Eva Carli was away and—

JEAN: I'll do Heinz and Vicars, but honestly, I can't do the abattoirs as well, it's on the other side of town…

Nasty pause.

ELLI: What about, Martin? He could sell at the abattoirs.

They all look at MARTIN.

MARTIN: Sure, sure.

GEORGE: How will he get out there?

MARTIN: I can ride out there…

GEORGE: You got a motorbike?

MARTIN: Pushbike.

GEORGE: It's ten miles.

MARTIN: That's okay.

FRANK: Morning and night.

MARTIN: That's okay.

Pause. They all look at him.

It's fine…

They all look at him for an oddly long moment.

GEORGE: I've got a man interested in a subscription… Richard Clark… Dickie Clark, at the railway workshop.

FRANK: Oh, yeah.

GEORGE: He's bought the paper five or six times. Seems quite a passionate young man.

FRANK: You know him, Martin?

MARTIN: What?

FRANK: You know this bloke…?

GEORGE: Dickie Clark…

MARTIN: No.

GEORGE: Railway workshop.

MARTIN: I don't get to the workshop much.

FRANK: You're in the yard, are you?

MARTIN: In the yard mainly, yeah…

ELLI: Are you a fitter and turner?

MARTIN: Yeah…

ELLI: You know Pauli Cecick?

MARTIN: Aah…

ELLI: He works in the yard.

MARTIN: Oh, yeah.

FRANK: Order. Maybe you could track him down, Martin. This…

GEORGE: Dickie Clark.

MARTIN: Sure.

FRANK: See, Martin, the way it goes is if he's interested enough to part
   with a couple of bob for the paper, he might be interested enough to
   come to meetings once a fortnight…

MARTIN: Uhuh.

FRANK: So have a chat to him… not like he wouldn't be welcome, is it?

   The others make agreeing noises.

When was the last time we went through the lists?

PHYLLIS: November…

   FRANK *looks at his watch.*

FRANK: That all right with everyone?

   People nod.

This time, though, we bite the bullet.

   Some people nod.

Anybody who's missed three meetings without a good reason, I don't
   care who they are, that's it, we don't re-issue them with cards, they're
   out, they're dead wood in my opinion.

ELLI: Maybe a warning letter.

FRANK: No. Bugger them. They've had enough letters. We don't want
   those sort of people in the Party. Phyll.

PHYLLIS: [*checking a list*] Um… Gwen Arlenson.

JEAN: She's sick I think.

PHYLLIS: Is she?

JEAN: I think she's sick.

PHYLLIS: I know her husband doesn't like her coming—

FRANK: Order. When was the last meeting she attended?

PHYLLIS: The fifth of February. She's not regular, but she's always there
   to hand out how-to-vote cards, and she never misses a fundraiser.

FRANK: She can do that stuff without being a member. Mark her down,
   Phyll. Who's next?

PHYLLIS: Petra and Misha Tamvakis. They last came to a meeting in November.

GEORGE: Well, we know why they're pissed off.

JEAN: I thought we decided they were out.

PHYLLIS: No we didn't.

JEAN: Petra talks too much.

ELLI: Who to?

JEAN: At the Federation. About the split, and all this other stuff. She shouldn't be talking about Party business to anyone, let alone to a group of—

FRANK: Order. She's missed more than three meetings without a valid excuse, so we'll withdraw her card and let the matter rest there.

GEORGE: What about Misha? He came to a meeting. I remember.

PHYLLIS: I've got him November as well.

GEORGE: We don't want to lose Misha. I know it's difficult but, augh… no, no… you wouldn't find a more hardworking, honest man than Misha. I think crazy to take his card. I'm sure he came to a meeting.

PHYLLIS: I'm sorry, George, he didn't come since last November or it would be written down here.

GEORGE: He came to a faction meeting.

FRANK: Did he?

GEORGE: Yeah… I think give him some time. He should keep his card.

General murmur of agreement.

ELLI: What about Petra?

GEORGE: Petra's different.

ELLI: If you take Petra's card away and let Misha keep his, that's not fair, I think someone should write them both a letter.

FRANK: They've been written a letter.

ELLI: Oh, come on, Frank. You know what I mean.

FRANK: Fine. Write them a letter… But don't go apologising about that little prick Sam Arnold. He's a nasty ultra-leftist with a foul mouth. I won't be called a bloody revisionist. Not at a fucking dinner dance. Who's next, Phyllis?

PHYLLIS: Brian Carli.

JEAN: And he's still doing it. He worms his way into people's houses and shows them his Chinese slides.

FRANK: Order.

JEAN: That's what happened with Petra and Misha.

GEORGE: Oh, come on, they're old friends.

FRANK: Order. Order.

PHYLLIS: Brian Carli.

GEORGE: Well, he hasn't been for a while.

FRANK: Cross him off.

PHYLLIS: Richard Hallem.

ELLI: He's moved to Horsham.

FRANK: All right, all right. Let's finish up… this is taking too long.

PHYLLIS: There's plenty more…

FRANK: Next time. Next time. Send them all letters. I don't care…

Pause. They all are a bit depressed.

PHYLLIS: We haven't welcomed Martin, officially I mean.

They all look at MARTIN. PHYLLIS *looks at* FRANK.

FRANK: As Secretary of the South Bendigo Branch of the Communist Party of Australia, I'd like to officially welcome Martin Porter to the Party.

Everyone claps. MARTIN *smiles.*

PHYLLIS: How did you become interested in Marxism, Martin?

MARTIN *keeps smiling. Everyone is looking at him.*

MARTIN: I… read stuff…

Everyone nods and smiles. Pause.

I think I saw, umm, the paper first and, you know, I thought… that looks good… you know…

Pause. People listen expectantly. MARTIN *is scared stiff.*

Everyone can see that working people get a raw deal, and the Russian idea, the Soviet idea of all pulling together and everyone equal and all that, I thought, I thought, you know, there's something in that… I thought, you know, like I thought, I should follow up on this, you know, we don't think about this stuff enough… the war… Vietnam, you know… and… um… the Aborigines, and, aaah, so… I went to the *Das Kapital* classes at the Mechanics Institute… and…

He shrugs.

FRANK: Good. I declare the meeting closed.

He gets up. Everyone starts getting up, collecting bags, etc.

ELLI: Would anyone like a cup of coffee, tea…?

PHYLLIS: No thanks, Elli.

JEAN: No I've / got to go.

> *They all start to leave.* MARTIN *is glued to his chair and feels sick.*

ELLI: Or a drink maybe… something stronger?

FRANK: Are you coming, Phyllis?

PHYLLIS: 'Bye.

ELLI: Really they shouldn't all run off like that, run off home like that… after your very first meeting. George?

GEORGE: Coffee.

ELLI: Martin, what would you like?

MARTIN: Aah…

ELLI: You all right?

> MARTIN *nods.*

You look sick.

> MARTIN *shakes his head.*

You all right…? George. This boy. He's sick.

GEORGE: You okay?

> MARTIN *nods, he is concentrating on not vomiting.*

ELLI: You want a cup of coffee? I make you a cup of coffee.

> MARTIN *shakes his head.*

You want something to eat?

> MARTIN *violently shakes his head.*

You going to be sick?

MARTIN: I'm fine.

> *He starts to get up.*

ELLI: You're going to be sick. George, he wants to be sick.

GEORGE: You feel sick?

MARTIN: No, I…

GEORGE: Be sick. Be sick. It's all right. Go on. Be sick.

MARTIN: No, I…

ELLI: He doesn't want to be sick on the floor.

GEORGE: Doesn't matter, just be sick.

ELLI: George.

GEORGE: It's a natural bodily function.

MARTIN: I'm sorry…

ELLI: It's all right… it's all right… Come on, Martin…

MARTIN: I'll just… I…

ELLI *comes over to him.*

ELLI: Come on… you're all right… you'll be all right…

She runs with him out of the room.

◆ ◆ ◆ ◆ ◆

SCENE NINE

MARTIN *is with* ALEX. *They are standing in grim silence.*

ALEX: Martin… don't worry about it…

MARTIN *doesn't reply.*

You threw up in their toilet. You're friends now.

MARTIN: Yeah, but why? Why was I so nervous? They must think it's suspicious… and I couldn't put two words together.

ALEX: That's all right.

MARTIN: I couldn't say why I wanted to be a communist. I don't want to be a communist.

ALEX: Of course you don't want to be a communist. No one in their right mind wants to be a communist.

MARTIN: I don't understand it.

ALEX: What don't you understand? Come on, we'll talk through it bit by bit.

MARTIN: No, it's not that.

ALEX: It's not what?

MARTIN: I understand it.

ALEX: Do you?

MARTIN: Yeah, I understand it.

ALEX: It makes sense to you, does it?

MARTIN: No.

ALEX: You think there just might just be something in it. Is that the problem?

MARTIN: No, no…

ALEX: Don't think it hasn't happened before. One of my best female agents, a twenty-year-old typist, gorgeous brunette, was brainwashed by a middle-aged Jewish communist, and ended up living in sin in Peking.

MARTIN: No…

ALEX: I've got a photograph of her in one of those little blue Mao suits. Fucking tragedy…

MARTIN: It's just I can't seem to lie… I can't pretend…

ALEX: You'll get better at it.

MARTIN: And they just seem so… normal. I mean, some of them, they're Greek and all that, but—

ALEX: Don't let them fool you, Martin. [*Pause*.] These people are traitors to their country. It's as simple as that. You know what position the communists took in the Second World War?

> MARTIN *shakes his head.*

They said if Russia became our enemy, they'd support Russia. Against their own country, Martin. They're zealots, and they've lost their humanity. Or, at the very least, they're naive. They're Russia's finger puppets. There's a war on, Martin. And Russian scientists are testing nuclear bombs in the Ukraine, and the people that seem so normal to you, are helping them. [*Pause*.] I'm going to do something now that's absolutely against my charter, but it's important you know what you're dealing with. I followed up on a few of the names you gave us, Martin.

> MARTIN *stares at him apprehensively.*

Frank Nash.

MARTIN: He's the Secretary.

ALEX: Believed to be identical with Arthur Francis Nash, member of the Communist Party of Australia since 1946. From 1946 to '49, while the Party was illegal, Arthur Nash worked as a cleaner at the Canberra War Memorial. [*Pause*.] What do you think he was doing at the War Memorial?

MARTIN: Cleaning…? I don't know. [*Pause*.] Can't anyone go to the War Memorial?

ALEX: Not to the basement… not to where they keep the files, the real stuff, Martin, top secret material about Australia's armed forces—

the Navy, Army, Air Force, you name it—numbers, names, battalions, roneoed copies of court martials, dishonourable discharges, memos between the allied powers, correspondence between leaders of nations, you want a communist nosing around in that stuff...?

MARTIN: Nah.

ALEX: You want a communist sending that lot off to his masters?

MARTIN: Nah.

ALEX: This is the other side of it, Martin. This is the side you don't see...

MARTIN *nods.*

He bobs up again in 1958, and this time he wants to be a history teacher. You're thinking what's wrong with that, yeah?

MARTIN: I...

ALEX: You know how many commie teachers there are out there, Martin, thousands, it's a policy they've got, it's written in their fucking constitution, infiltrate the schools, across the board, state schools,

Tom Long (left) as Martin and Steve Le Marquand as Alex in the 2004 Company B production. (Photo: Heidrun Löhr)

private schools, breed a whole generation of people that think like them, and look how well it's worked, look at the fucking students, pissing on the cops, sitting down in the middle of the fucking road...

    MARTIN *nods*.

He calls himself Frank instead of Arthur. He gets a bit depressed. His wife leaves him, can't stand his fanaticism. And he moves to Bathurst, miles away. He gets this little group together, in Bathurst, in 1962, a Communist Front, they call themselves the Bathurst Municipal Library Association, three of the eight-member group are known communists... and they agitate to start a library. He meets Phyllis Agnes Platten, a primary school teacher with left leanings, and he commences an adulterous relationship with her.

MARTIN: Phyll... she was married?

ALEX: Oh, yeah, she was married. He bought her copies of Marx and Engels, he told her all about class struggle, they fucked on the desk in her classroom after hours, he brainwashed her, Martin, and she left her husband and joined the Party. In 1963, they visit the Soviet Union, Yugoslavia, Poland, Czechoslovakia and the German Democratic Republic, and when they come back to Australia, they move to Bendigo... He's a louse. He's a communist agitator, and he's a menace to society... You've told your fiancée, haven't you?

    MARTIN *nods*.

What's she going to think if you drop out now? [*Pause*.] And you're on the payroll. You're in the house. You've done your first meeting. It's the hardest one. Don't be a mug, Martin.

◆ ◆ ◆ ◆ ◆

SCENE TEN

ANNETTE *and* TRIXIE *are sitting in the living room.* TRIXIE *has a swathe of white satin on her knee. She is sewing in big angry loops.* ANNETTE *is watching her apprehensively.*

ANNETTE: I'll do it, Trix.
TRIXIE: No, no. I'll do it.

    Pause. ANNETTE *goes to leave.*

Don't you run off. I want to talk to you.

ANNETTE *sits down.*

So when exactly did you decide you didn't want to be married in the church?

ANNETTE: About a month ago.

TRIXIE: And you didn't think to tell me?

ANNETTE: We thought it would be—

TRIXIE: Whose idea was it?

ANNETTE: It was… Martin's idea.

TRIXIE: And you just said yes.

ANNETTE: I didn't say yes immediately.

TRIXIE: How long did you take?

ANNETTE: We talked about it for a few days.

TRIXIE: So you argued?

ANNETTE: No we didn't argue. We talked.

TRIXIE: What did you talk about?

ANNETTE: Trix, can you be a bit careful with the…

TRIXIE *rips the thread off with her teeth.*

We talked about how it would cause… upset…

ANNETTE *is getting a bit upset herself.*

… and I talked about how I'd always wanted to get married in the church… and then Martin talked about his beliefs… and I said I wanted to think about it for a night, and I thought about it, and I said all right, that I didn't mind.

TRIXIE: I don't believe you.

ANNETTE: It's true. I don't mind.

TRIXIE: Why don't you mind? It's just beyond me that you wouldn't mind.

ANNETTE: I dunno.

TRIXIE: Are you feeling guilty about something? Have you and Martin been… having…?

ANNETTE: No. I just don't mind.

TRIXIE: Have you told your parents?

ANNETTE: Yes, we told them last night.

TRIXIE: What do they think about it? They're furious, aren't they? I'm going to ring your mother up.

ANNETTE: Oh no, Trix, please don't. We've made our mind up. Can't
   you—
TRIXIE: I don't think you understand, Annette. This is not some little
   decision you and Martin can just make. Don't you care what you're
   doing to your parents?
ANNETTE: Yes, but—
TRIXIE: You're making a laughing stock of us all in front of the whole
   town.
ANNETTE: At least we're getting married.
TRIXIE: I think that would be better. On the scale of things. I think that
   would be better.
ANNETTE: Oh, Trix.
TRIXIE: No, I mean it. I could cope with you living in sin. For a couple
   of months. If you didn't tell anybody, but this, this is different, this
   is an outright rejection of the church.
ANNETTE: Martin believes very strongly in it.
TRIXIE: In what?
ANNETTE: In… communism.

   Pause. They are both almost crying.

TRIXIE: Talk to him, Annette. Tell him he can't do this.
ANNETTE: I can't.
TRIXIE: Refuse to marry him. Say you won't marry him unless it's
   properly, in the church.

   ANNETTE *shakes her head.*

Talk to Father Michael. Just talk to him.

   ANNETTE *says nothing.*

Are you like him? Is that what it is?
ANNETTE: No I'm not.
TRIXIE: What are your family's politics?
ANNETTE: I don't want to go into it.
TRIXIE: Yes you do.
ANNETTE: I don't know… We don't talk about it.
TRIXIE: Of course you know. Of course you know your family's politics.
ANNETTE: They vote for the Labor Party.
TRIXIE: I see…
ANNETTE: Dad's always been Labor.

TRIXIE: I would've thought being Catholic, they would at least vote for the DLP.

ANNETTE: He doesn't like the DLP.

TRIXIE: Why?

ANNETTE: He thinks they're anti-union.

TRIXIE: I wouldn't have said it's the unions they're against. I would've said—

ANNETTE: Look, I didn't bring this up.

TRIXIE: Martin never mentioned any of this.

ANNETTE: Any of what?

TRIXIE: Is your father a communist?

ANNETTE: No.

TRIXIE: Some of them are in the Labor Party.

ANNETTE: Well, he's not.

TRIXIE: Has Martin been talking to him?

ANNETTE: He's not a communist!

TRIXIE: Well, where did Martin get these ideas then? He's never been interested in politics or anything. He was in the air cadets at school, he played trumpet in the CMF, and marched, got up six o'clock in the morning and marched, and we always voted for Mr Menzies, except for one time, one time in 1961 we didn't, but all the rest, and he was a lovely boy, Martin, he was a lovely patriotic boy with short hair and now look at him.

◆ ◆ ◆ ◆ ◆

SCENE ELEVEN

1967. Communist Party sub-meeting at Elli and George's house. MARTIN *is reading from a document. He has sideburns and long hair down to his shoulders.*

MARTIN: [*reading*] 'We should not fear debate in the Party if it is to elucidate problems, improve our work and is conducted within the limits of democratic centralism.'

GEORGE: Well, that's pretty clear.

ELLI: Yes it's clear, but…

GEORGE: What? Come on.

ELLI: Well, it's not going to happen, is it?

GEORGE: Why not?

ELLI: We can go through all these points and make recommendations to our hearts' content, but Frank is the Secretary, and he's not going to change.

GEORGE: The Party says he has to change. The Party says meetings must be fun.

> *They laugh.*

MARTIN: Like the Girls Friendly Society.

> *They laugh.*

GEORGE: Frank'll cope.

ELLI: [*in Greek*] Yes… [*then in English*] like he coped with all the Chinese stuff.

GEORGE: Don't be disrespectful

ELLI: Oh, come on, it was funny—

MARTIN: We do have to get through these points.

ELLI: Well, what will I put for that one?

GEORGE: It's clear… just read it out, freer debate, blah, blah blah.

MARTIN: How about when we have the reports, instead of one, two people present reports on the same subject, like… say… anti-Semitism in the Soviet Union… but from different perspectives?

ELLI: That's good.

GEORGE: That's stupid.

ELLI: Why is that stupid?

GEORGE: You're manufacturing an argument. Like some bourgeois debating club. Discussion should just bubble up naturally or it shouldn't happen at all.

MARTIN: Yes, but it doesn't happen at all, that's what the problem is.

GEORGE: Well, maybe it doesn't need to happen, then.

ELLI: So you think this whole thing is stupid?

GEORGE: No, I think it's good. I like what Aarons and all them have to say. I think they're seduced by the Italians and I certainly don't think the Italians have all the answers.

ELLI: What's wrong with the Italians?

GEORGE: There's nothing wrong with them. I just don't think they're perfect.

MARTIN: They've got thirty percent membership.

GEORGE: They're Europeans. Half of them were sung to sleep with 'The Internationale'. It's different here. A Party needs some discipline.

ELLI: So you don't think there should be discussion.

GEORGE: Of course I think there should be discussion.

ELLI: Good.

> ELLI *writes down on her paper.* PHYLLIS *enters. They all look up.*

PHYLLIS: Am I early?

ELLI: No.

GEORGE: No, no, we just lost track of the time…

> FRANK *enters.* PHYLLIS *and* FRANK *take off their coats and sit down at the table.* ELLI *gives* MARTIN *the notes she has made.*

MARTIN: You want / me to read this?

FRANK: I didn't see you on Sunday.

GEORGE: No, I'm sorry, the shop. I just couldn't get away. How many turned up in the end?

PHYLLIS: Thirty, thirty-five, it was good.

> *Pause.* FRANK *glances through the agenda, then looks at his watch.*

FRANK: I declare this meeting open. Apologies…

PHYLLIS: Mick Leavis, Edna Cortese, Paul Ryan, Michael Petit, Lance Whitney, Gwen Arlinson, Blackie Nugent, Polly Nugent, Rex Place, Lorna Pierce, Yanni Costas, Craig and Agnes Pitt, Rupert Pollet, Maisie Pollet, Alan Tremaine.

GEORGE: And Manni's not coming.

FRANK: Any correspondence…

> JEAN *enters, quickly takes off her coat, and takes a seat.*

PHYLLIS: A few things have come in… Some copies of a book people might like to look at—*Children of Vietnam*—it's pretty rough stuff… They're… fifty cents each. We can order however many we want and sell them at the stall on Saturday.

FRANK: Jean, perhaps you could take care of that.

PHYLLIS: … And there's a possibility the Soviet Friendship Society might tour their current film bill, *Interrupted Melody*—Soviet and Czech soldiers in the battle against fascism—and *Untried Youth*—

pages from the lives of young builders of communism. They want to know if we could get a hall and if we could get a crowd in. Well, I s'pose they want to know if it's financially worth their while…

FRANK: How many did we get last time?

ELLI: It was a good turnout last time, fifty or sixty.

PHYLLIS: That was the outer-space film, that was very—

FRANK: Order. Just reassure them we can get a crowd in. Perhaps, Jean, you could take care of that. All right. What's next?

PHYLLIS: The membership initiative from the national office.

FRANK: Did you make any sense of it?

MARTIN: Well, we've gone through their points one by one and tried to come up with recommendations.

Everyone nods.

Shall I just read them?

Everyone nods.

[*Reading*] 'In order that the meetings be brighter and more lively, it is recommended that members ensure they are not over-tired when they come to meetings, that they approach the meetings not as boring necessities, but as opportunities to engage in lively and passionate debate with their like-minded comrades, that they read all the reports and the latest copy of the paper so they are up with the latest developments and can contribute to the meetings, that food and drink, including wines and beers, not just teas and coffee, are served after the meeting, and members are encouraged not to dash off home like they have to get home to their mothers after the meetings finish, but to stay and engage in free discussion of the issues of the time, that in the meetings themselves less emphasis will be put on selling the paper, or how important it is to sell the paper, who has sold how many copies, who has devoted the most time to selling, people's shortcomings as papersellers, and how they might overcome them and be better papersellers, and the sombre, severe, one might even say Stalinist atmosphere should be replaced by a happier, friendlier feel, and time put aside for discussion…'

◆ ◆ ◆ ◆ ◆

SCENE TWELVE

A few hours later. ELLI, GEORGE *and* MARTIN *have kept drinking and talking after the meeting.*

ELLI: He was in the Communist Party but he worked for the EDA, the United Democratic Left. He was very pompous.

GEORGE: I was not.

ELLI: He knew all the famous people, and he dropped their names casually into the conversation.

GEORGE: I did not.

ELLI: Like Lambrakis, he knew Lambrakis, who was assassinated in '63. Have you heard of him?

MARTIN: Nope.

ELLI: He was very famous, even more so after he died. Hugely famous. And Theodorakis. You must have heard of him?

MARTIN: Sorry.

ELLI: Anyway, George used to get his hair cut at my father's barber's shop. His father knew my father. They were both communists, but George's father was like communist aristocracy. Papa Zannos knew Lenin.

GEORGE *tries not to look smug.*

So that's how we met. Very romantic. Surrounded by bits of snipped-off hair. He'd always get the same cut, very short all over, but this long piece of hair growing down his back, just here. It was more than a foot long…

GEORGE: Oh, bullshit.

ELLI: … trailing down his back like something he'd forgotten, it looked so bad, every time it got longer and longer, but then one afternoon, my father accidentally cut it off.

MARTIN: Oh, no.

GEORGE: It was no accident.

ELLI: My father was too embarrassed to tell him so he put the piece of hair in his pocket and he said to George, 'Why do you leave this piece of hair at the back so long, shall I cut it off for you?' and George became very serious and said—

GEORGE: This is all bullshit. This is so much bullshit.

ELLI: [*in Greek*] 'No, Lefteri, that piece of hair, I am growing it for my country, and I'll only cut it off when Greece is liberated, and my people are united.'

MARTIN: What does it mean?

ELLI: 'No, Lefteri, that piece of hair, I am growing it for my country, and I'll only cut it off when Greece is liberated, and my people are united.' And my father nodded, and they hugged each other with tears in their eyes, and he left the shop... without his hair! The piece of hair was in my father's pocket, and we didn't know what to do, whether we should mail it back to him in an envelope, 'cause we didn't think he'd ever come back, but a month later, he walks in, like nothing has happened, and he gets his usual cut... And then he got put into jail again. And they shaved all his hair off.

> ELLI *pours out more drinks for everyone.*

MARTIN: Why did they put you in jail?

GEORGE: The country was at war, it was civil war between the left and the right. Thousands of communists were thrown into jail. Thousands murdered.

MARTIN: Is this after the World War?

GEORGE: Of course. After the occupation. And the fucking British! Greece would be a communist country today, but the British and the Americans installed the right-wing Safoulis government to crush the communists. Just like they're doing in Vietnam.

MARTIN: Is that why you came here?

GEORGE: No... that was before we came... we came later...

ELLI: George was a marked man, you know. It got so we couldn't go anywhere. It was ridiculous. So we came here.

MARTIN: What year was that?

GEORGE: 1957.

ELLI: And George had to use his cousin's name, Tassakis, that's the name on his passport...

GEORGE: [*in Greek*] Elena, what are you doing? Don't talk about this.

ELLI: [*in Greek*] Don't worry, he's like a son. [*In English*] They're bastards, the Australian immigration people, they nose out all the communists. Nazis, no worries, come right in, but communists... Why do we never see Annette?

MARTIN: You see her, don't you?

ELLI: You're not proud of her.

MARTIN: I'm… No, I'm… very proud of her…

> GEORGE *has been putting on a record. He turns it up loud and talks loudly over the top.* ELLI *fills up everyone's drinks.*

GEORGE: This is Theodorakis. He is a communist.

MARTIN: It's very stirring.

GEORGE: I beg your pardon?

MARTIN: It's very stirring.

GEORGE: Yes… You like it?

MARTIN: Yeah.

> *A woman sings. The song is passionate and moving.*

ELLI: Maria Farantouri.

> *They listen for a moment.*

GEORGE: Very good composer. He is in jail. His music is banned. You cannot play it in Greece.

MARTIN: Really?

GEORGE: You get arrested for playing his music.

MARTIN: Bloody hell.

> GEORGE *turns it down.*

GEORGE: As if you can ban music. It's like something out of a fairytale. A corrupt old king who wants to stop the people singing.

ELLI: Like Stalin.

GEORGE: I think that's a bit different.

ELLI: No it's not, Georgo.

GEORGE: It is a bit different.

ELLI: It's not any different.

GEORGE: Why do you want to talk about Stalin? You always want to talk about Stalin.

ELLI: I don't want to talk about Stalin.

GEORGE: You're worse than a bloody conservative. You want to leave the Party?

ELLI: No I don't want to leave the Party.

GEORGE: Well, shut up, then.

ELLI: I just said he didn't like music.

GEORGE: He did like music.

MARTIN: He didn't like Shostakovich.

GEORGE: What have you been reading?

ELLI: I lent it to him. He should know the history of the Party.

GEORGE: Which version? Trotsky's?

MARTIN: He hated his fourth symphony.

GEORGE: That was Zhdanov.

MARTIN: He said it quacked and grunted and growled.

ELLI: Now what does that sound like?

GEORGE: Elli.

ELLI: Someone having sex, that's what it sounds like.

GEORGE: Elli.

ELLI: They were squeamish about sex. The lot of them.

GEORGE: No one wants to hear you talking like that! This is ancient history. And anyway, you've got it all wrong. As usual. They wanted people fucking. They got over all that early morality stuff, and in the thirties they wanted everybody fucking.

ELLI: Yes, well they still didn't like Shostakovich.

GEORGE: Who cares. They didn't ban him.

ELLI: They may as well have.

GEORGE: But they didn't.

ELLI: No, they did worse things than ban music.

GEORGE: This has been talked about enough.

ELLI: That's why Czechoslovakia is so important. Isn't it, Martin?

MARTIN: Don't bring me into this.

ELLI: Communism has to shift. There's something dead about it. Something sick.

GEORGE: Don't talk like that.

ELLI: It's dull and vicious, defending itself all the time, like a siege mentality—

GEORGE: Well, of course they've got a siege mentality.

ELLI: Maybe they suffered too much in the war. Maybe they're all mad.

    ELLI *has been looking for a record. She finds it.*

GEORGE: [*in Greek*] You're being very irresponsible in front of an impressionable young man.

    She puts it on. Shostakovich floods the room.

ELLI: Is it so decadent?

GEORGE: I never said it was decadent. I just don't like it.

ELLI: Why don't you like it?
GEORGE: I just don't like it. But I never said no one can play it.
  He takes the record off.
ELLI: What are you doing?
GEORGE: I'm putting Theodorakis back on.
ELLI: I want Martin to hear Shostakovich.
GEORGE: We were listening to Theodorakis. You took my record off.
ELLI: Your record had finished.
GEORGE: It had not finished.
ELLI: Theodorakis wouldn't want to be set up as the proper communist
  alternative to Shostakovich.
GEORGE: How do you know?
ELLI: I bet he wouldn't.
GEORGE: You've never even met him.
ELLI: I'm going to write to him and ask him whether he likes Shostakovich.
GEORGE: I've met him. I've drunk with him. I've played music with him.
ELLI: What music have you played with him?
GEORGE: I have sung a song accompanied by Mikis on the guitar. He
  told me. He doesn't like Shostakovich.
ELLI: You liar.
GEORGE: What do you want to listen to, Martin? Theodorakis or
  Shostakovich?
ELLI: Oh, don't be stupid.
GEORGE: You have no Party mindfulness.
ELLI: You have no Party mindfulness.
GEORGE: Martin?
MARTIN: I really don't mind.
GEORGE: Martin doesn't mind.

◆ ◆ ◆ ◆ ◆

SCENE THIRTEEN

MARTIN *is sitting talking into his tape recorder a couple of hours later.
He talks fast and smooth and chain-smokes. It is three-thirty in the
morning.*

MARTIN: Frank Nash is pissed off about the push from the Executive to
  be more friendly and democratic. He thinks it's all a bit immature.

Still, he can't help but do as Taft and the rest say, so there was a stilted discussion about the developments in Czechoslovakia. Opinion is divided about whether it's moving away from socialism, or whether it's the new road forward. Jean and Frank are very suspicious of it, despite the glowing descriptions in the *Trib*. There's talk of Taft or some other Party big shot coming to a meeting in a few months and filling us in on the latest stuff from the Soviet Union, the stuff that can't be written in the paper or put in the mail, Frank said. Phyllis and Frank are bickering all the time now, even at meetings. Jean Bennett found out she didn't get the library job at UNICEF, and I overheard her telling Phyll that it's spooks that are doing it—

Someone knocks on the door. MARTIN *stops abruptly.*

ANNETTE: [*offstage*] Martin.

MARTIN: Yeah.

ANNETTE: [*offstage*] Can I come in?

MARTIN: I've just got to finish this... sorry...

Pause. ANNETTE *opens the door a crack and looks in.*

ANNETTE: When did you get back?

MARTIN: About half an hour ago...

ANNETTE: Where were you? It's half past three.

MARTIN: I was just at the meeting... and talking after...

Pause.

ANNETTE: Are you coming to bed?

MARTIN: In a minute.

ANNETTE *walks away.* MARTIN *switches his tape recorder back on to record.*

Something interesting came up about George Tassakis. Tassakis is not his real name. He assumed the name of his cousin in order to get into Australia because he was a member of the Greek Communist Party and something called the United Democratic Left, and he's been in jail. He worked with a man called Lambakis or Lambrakus in the late fifties, an insurgent who died in dramatic circumstances, and who has a cult following. I can't be sure... but I think his real name is George Zannos.

◆ ◆ ◆ ◆ ◆

SCENE FOURTEEN

ELLI *and* GEORGE *are hosting a dinner for Martin's birthday, with* FRANK, MARTIN *and* ANNETTE.

FRANK: Aren't you just a little sick of all the adulation they're getting, page after bloody page in the *Tribune*? It's all that's in it.

ELLI: Don't you want to read about it?

FRANK: All those sideswipes at the Soviet Union, like they're still in some sort of communist dark ages... like they're a bloody dinosaur.

GEORGE: They haven't quite said that.

FRANK: And the bloody leadership won't tell us anything. How are we meant to know what's going on?

ELLI: No, they don't tell us enough.

FRANK: They're all bloody intellectuals, bloody Jewish intellectuals.

MARTIN: Jesus, Frank, come on...

FRANK: Yeah, well I'm sick of these middle-class bludgers running the Party. Never done a day's work in their lives.

GEORGE: That's not true.

FRANK: It is true, it didn't used to be true, but it's true now.

MARTIN: It's the same in Russia.

FRANK: No it's not. I've been there, and it's not.

ELLI: No, they've sidelined the intellectuals in Russia.

FRANK: Why are you even in the Communist Party if you're so critical of the Soviet Union?

ELLI: Because I'm a communist.

FRANK: Are you? If there's a dig to be made, you'll make it.

GEORGE: Oh, come on, Frank. You have criticisms—

FRANK: I might be critical of them, but I'm not ashamed of them.

> PHYLLIS *enters with a parcel.*

PHYLLIS: [*to* MARTIN] Happy birthday.

> *She gives* MARTIN *his parcel.*

Open it. Open it.

> *It is a bright red jumper. They all laugh. He puts it on.*

FRANK: I like the choice of colour.

GEORGE: He's unmistakable now.

They laugh. PHYLLIS *sits down. Pause.*

ELLI: Now if only you'd join the Party, Annette, we could start the meeting.

They laugh.

ANNETTE: I'm quite interested in joining the Party.

ELLI: Oh.

ANNETTE: But Martin doesn't want me to.

MARTIN: You've never said you wanted to join the Party.

ANNETTE: I know I've never said—

MARTIN: I didn't think you were interested in politics.

ANNETTE: Well, it's hard to avoid them round our house.

GEORGE: No one should avoid politics. Martin, you should be thrilled about this. This is fantastic news.

FRANK: It often happens this way.

PHYLLIS: Let's be honest, it's how the party bloody grows, we're like rabbits. Young male communist rabbits bringing lots of lady rabbits into the burrow.

They all laugh except FRANK.

FRANK: Don't be trivial, Phyllis.

PHYLLIS: I just was saying what you said.

FRANK: You make it sound like there's no politics involved, no beliefs or anything.

ANNETTE: Just rabbits wanting to root other rabbits.

They laugh.

PHYLLIS: I didn't mean that. Of course there's beliefs involved.

FRANK: Or is it just a social club for you, love?

GEORGE: I think it's an important point. So does Mr Menzies. That's why he built a rabbit-proof fence.

They laugh.

FRANK: That wasn't Menzies. That was last century.

GEORGE: Well, the other stuff, the chemical stuff.

ANNETTE: Mixo.

ELLI: You should come to a meeting.

ANNETTE: Do you think?

ELLI: Shouldn't she, Martin?

MARTIN: Yeah, of course.

ANNETTE: I'd feel so ignorant.

GEORGE: You come to my night classes. I'll teach you.

ANNETTE: What do you teach?

GEORGE: Marxist economics.

ANNETTE: Well, I know about capitalist economics, 'cause I run a hairdressing salon.

They laugh.

GEORGE: That's not so silly. I learn an enormous amount from our shop. And Marx, Karl Marx learnt about capitalism from his father's business. Of course it makes it harder for you in the Party, you have to carry the stigma of being a petit bourgeois, in the shopkeeper class—

ELLI: Georgo.

GEORGE: But we're allowed to, 'cause we're Greek, we're very good with money. Do you own the hairdressers?

ANNETTE: No I manage it.

GEORGE: Well then, you're a wage-earner.

FRANK: No she's not. She's a manager.

GEORGE: She's getting paid.

FRANK: She gets paid to manage.

ANNETTE: And I do people's hair.

PHYLLIS: She's a foreman.

MARTIN: She's a hairdresser.

GEORGE: You're a manager, Frank.

FRANK: I'm not a manager.

GEORGE: You have people underneath you. Isn't that a manager?

FRANK: I'm head of a section.

ELLI: My father was a barber.

ANNETTE: Was he?

ELLI: I grew up in a barber's shop.

ANNETTE: Where do you get your hair cut?

ELLI: I cut it myself.

ANNETTE *sizes up her hair.*

ANNETTE: Not bad.

PHYLLIS *giggles.*

FRANK: Oh really, can you can go into the kitchen if you're going to talk about personal grooming?

ANNETTE: I'm at Dawn Hair and Beauty, in Booth Street, off the square.

ELLI: I'll keep that in mind.

ANNETTE: We could talk about politics.

ELLI: If you want to—

FRANK: You've got great cadre here, Martin.

MARTIN: Yeah…

FRANK: Why this sudden enthusiasm for politics, Annette?

ANNETTE: I've decided there's two ways of thinking and you've got to choose which one you believe in.

GEORGE: Bravo.

ANNETTE: It's become very clear to me… because of the reading I've been doing.

FRANK: What have you been giving her, Martin?

ANNETTE: I've been reading about Kim Philby. In the papers.

Pause.

FRANK: I'm not sure what you mean.

ANNETTE: You know, Kim Philby, the third man.

FRANK: He was a spy for the Soviet Union. Is that what you want to be?

ANNETTE: No…

MARTIN: Annette, don't bore everyone with—

ANNETTE: But he's a communist, isn't he?

FRANK: He's an upper-class English communist who spied for the Soviet Union. We're the Australian Communist Party. I'm not quite sure what you're getting at.

MARTIN: She's just—

ANNETTE: Don't you like him?

FRANK: I don't not like him. He's not my hero if that's what you mean.

ANNETTE: Who are your heroes?

FRANK: I prefer people who openly declare their politics and fight for them.

PHYLLIS: Frank's his own hero.

ANNETTE: Me and Martin can't get enough of Kim Philby. It's such an amazing story. We've been buying every paper, haven't we Marty, every bloody paper to find out the latest thing…

Awkward pause.

MARTIN: Well, it… it is an amazing story… what he got away with…

Pause.

GEORGE: But he got caught, didn't he?

ANNETTE: No, no, he didn't. He got away, but they didn't tell anybody till now, he lives in a huge apartment in Moscow and he's been given all these Soviet decorations and everything, after having to live a lie all his life, from when he was at Cambridge University as a student… it's so amazing. His wife went over there, Eleanor Philby, she went to live in Moscow, even though she'd never known he'd been a spy. Some spies never tell their wives. They never tell anybody. They live tragic lives, never able to be who they really are—

MARTIN: Annette—

ANNETTE: That was the amazing thing, that he didn't get caught, though he nearly got caught, didn't he, Marty, so close, when he was working in Vienna and there was a man who flew in from Russia on a plane, a defector, to tell him that he had information that could lead to the third man… but what he didn't know was that he was talking to the third man, imagine that, and so Philby… was able to get rid of him…

Pause.

GEORGE: The class system in England, eh, they couldn't believe that one of their own would betray them so thoroughly.

FRANK: I think it's wise to be careful when you're talking about this cloak and dagger bullshit.

ANNETTE: But it's all in the paper. Anyone can read it.

FRANK: Yeah, I know, but you don't want to play into their hands, do you?

ANNETTE: Whose hands?

MARTIN: The spooks.

Pause.

ANNETTE: The what?

FRANK: The secret police, we've got them in this country, you know. ASIO…

Everyone is quiet. It's not a word that is mentioned very often.

They tap people's phones, they stop people getting jobs, they ruin people's lives. They masquerade as communists and join branches. And the thing they most love is a spurious fucking connection between a legitimate political party and fucking espionage.

PHYLLIS: Frank…

FRANK: I don't mean to be rude, Annette, but you're married to a member of the Communist Party, and I don't know what you go talking about in your hairdressing shop there, but if these things get mixed up like they're one and the same thing, like they did with Petrov, then people's lives get hurt, and the Party gets damaged, and I don't think it's worth it for an interesting dinner party conversation, do you? [*Pause.*] And I would've thought you'd had more sense too, Martin.

GEORGE: Oh, come on. We've all been fascinated by it. What's the harm?

    ANNETTE *starts to cry.*

ANNETTE: I'm sorry. I'm so sorry.

    Pause. MARTIN *puts his arm around her.*

MARTIN: Heh, heh, it's all right…

George Spartels as George and Eugenia Fragos as Elli in the 2004 Company B production. (Photo: Heidrun Löhr)

ELLI: Jesus, Frank, you're a nasty bastard. She just likes reading the paper, that's all she was doing, reading the paper and getting excited.

GEORGE: You apologise to her. She's a guest in my house. You apologise to her.

◆ ◆ ◆ ◆ ◆

SCENE FIFTEEN

A couple of hours later. Back at their house.

MARTIN: I can't believe you did that.

ANNETTE: I didn't do anything.

MARTIN: You fucking did.

ANNETTE: I didn't do anything. They liked me.

MARTIN: They thought you were a fool.

ANNETTE: No they didn't.

MARTIN: Bursting into tears in front of everybody.

ANNETTE: They didn't mind. They liked me.

MARTIN: Who cares if they liked you?

ANNETTE: Who else have I got to be friends with, Martin?

MARTIN: You can't be friends with them.

ANNETTE: Nobody wants to know us. None of our friends like us anymore.

MARTIN: I know it's—

ANNETTE: You go round organising anti-war demonstrations, maybe it'd be all right in the city, but in Bendigo, twenty people come, people think you're a fruit loop. And I'm married to you.

MARTIN: More than twenty people come.

ANNETTE: Who have I got to be friends with?

MARTIN: You can't be friends with them.

ANNETTE: Well, why do I have to have dinner with them, then?

MARTIN: Keep your voice down. Fucking raving on about spying, fucking Kim Philby, what are you, crazy? Do you want me to get caught? Is that what you want?

ANNETTE: No, of course not.

MARTIN: Well, what were you doing?

ANNETTE: They didn't think anything.

MARTIN: How do you know?

ANNETTE: I could tell they didn't.

MARTIN: How do you know Frank's not talking to Melbourne at this very fucking minute?

ANNETTE: I don't reckon he is. I think I'm better at it than you are. You just sat there like a stunned mullet.

MARTIN: What was I meant to do?

ANNETTE: I would've thought you'd be smoother than that.

MARTIN: How, smoother?

ANNETTE: Well, just taken it a bit more in your stride. Smoked a cigarette and laughed and stuff... Talked in a low voice like you do when you're sitting in the spare room by yourself.

> *Pause.*

MARTIN: I don't smoke with them.

ANNETTE: What do you mean?

MARTIN: They don't know I smoke.

ANNETTE: Why is that such a big secret?

MARTIN: It just helps, that's all.

ANNETTE: Helps with what?

MARTIN: Helps me remember stuff.

> *Pause.* MARTIN *gets out a cigarette and lights it.*

ANNETTE: You're the wrong class to be a spy. That's your problem. Middle-class people are spies.

MARTIN: That's bullshit.

ANNETTE: You don't do it right.

> *Pause.*

MARTIN: Well, we won't do it again, don't worry about that. No more dinner parties... And if she comes into your hairdressers you fucking give her a bad haircut and overcharge her.

ANNETTE: That won't stop her. She likes me.

MARTIN: Stay away from her.

ANNETTE: I could find out things for you. People talk in hairdressers.

MARTIN: Don't be fucking stupid. You're not the fucking spy. I'm the spy. I'm the spy.

ANNETTE: What makes you any better at it than me?

MARTIN: Now you want to be a spy. Is that it?

ANNETTE: Maybe I want to be a spy, or maybe I want to join the Party.

MARTIN: Oh, bullshit.

ANNETTE: Yeah, well I'm not as bloody right-wing as you are.

MARTIN: I'm not right-wing.

ANNETTE: You are. You're a bloody spy, for God's sake.

MARTIN: Spies aren't necessarily right-wing.

ANNETTE: Your sort is. Writing down lists of mothers at the mothers' club.

MARTIN: How would you know?

ANNETTE: You left it on the kitchen table, some spy you are.

MARTIN: Look, I don't care why you want to do it, you're not joining the Party.

ANNETTE: Well, what else am I meant to do? I've got nothing to do, there's nothing to do, you're at meetings every night. I'm bored, Martin. I'm bored.

MARTIN: Read a book. Go round to Mum's.

ANNETTE: Oh, yeah, that'd be fun.

MARTIN: Well, what do you want me to do?

ANNETTE: I want you to stop.

MARTIN: You don't stop doing something like this, Annette. I wish to God I'd never told you.

ANNETTE: You couldn't wait to tell me. Not like Kim Philby. Kim Philby kept it a secret from his wife. She didn't have to worry about it all the bloody time. Kim Phiby went and worked overseas and—

MARTIN: Shut up about Kim Phiby. Shut the fuck up about Kim Philby. He's on the other side, for God's sake... I'm good at it, you know. I can split my brain into two compartments, and when I'm in one compartment, it feels like it's real, I'm a whole person, I'm just using half my brain but I look like a whole person, and it comes out natural. I'll tell you something, Annette, I'll tell you something, when I'm with the Party, when I'm at meetings, the smell of a cigarette makes me sick, the smoke makes me physically sick, but when I'm at home, when I'm with you, just round the house, I crave it, I smoke them one after the other. How do you explain that? It's uncanny, don't you reckon, what the body can do. Alex says he's never come across it, in fifteen years he's never seen anything like it and he deals with hundreds of spies. I'm good at it, I know I am,

I'm better than Kim Philby. You think they like you, you think you had a little success with the communists at the dinner party, well I'll tell you what, they love me, Annette, they love me…

END OF ACT ONE

ACT TWO: 1968

SCENE ONE

MARTIN *approaches* ALEX, *who is reading a newspaper in the park.*

MARTIN: Thanks for coming.

ALEX: What's so important?

MARTIN: I gotta talk to you about Czechoslovakia.

ALEX: What about it? I've only got a few minutes.

MARTIN: Did you get my last report?

ALEX: Yeah.

MARTIN: Did you read it?

ALEX: Yeah.

MARTIN: Alex I think the branch is gonna split. I think it's going to happen at the next meeting.

ALEX: Oh, yeah.

MARTIN: Frank's got himself way out on a limb. He's scrabbling around for support but he's not getting much. Jean waivers this way, then that way—

ALEX: What's your problem, Marty?

MARTIN: Frank wants everyone to sign this resolution to the Executive in Sydney saying that the human face of communism stuff is all bullshit, that the Czech's are counter-revolutionary, and that if things keep going the way they are, the West Germans, backed by the Americans, are going to move into Czechoslovakia, and that'll be the end of communism.

   ALEX *laughs.*

So should I sign it? See I don't think I should.

ALEX: Ahuh.

MARTIN: Partly because I'm more aligned with the reformists.

ALEX: Right.

MARTIN: But also because I'm in the perfect position to encourage the split. I could move a vote of no confidence in the Secretary. I could topple Frank.

ALEX *doesn't say anything.*

Alex?

ALEX: It's all bullshit, Martin. It's all bullshit.

MARTIN: What do you mean?

ALEX: They'll stick with the Soviet Union. Go with Frank.

MARTIN: But the Party's—

ALEX: They'll stick with the Soviet Union.

MARTIN: Have you looked at the *Tribune* lately, Alex?

ALEX: I don't need to read their paper, Marty. I got a direct line.

MARTIN: I feel like if I go with Frank, I'll be out of the Party, like the ones who went off with China, and now they've got their own Party, the Marxist Leninists.

ALEX: Yeah, I know about them, Martin.

MARTIN: Well, then I won't be any use, I'll be out of the Party. I'll be in this other Party. How can I tell you anything if I'm out of the Party?

ALEX: Calm down, Marty.

MARTIN: I feel like I've got a real place there now… I feel like I could get elected to some position or something, Treasurer or something, not Secretary necessarily, but if Frank goes, there will be an opening…

ALEX *doesn't seem madly impressed.*

Shouldn't I be encouraging the split?

ALEX: Maybe… I'm not quite sure what we gain from it.

MARTIN: If I became Secretary, Alex, I could get you stuff about the whole Southern Region, I could get you books full of names, but I got to play my cards right, I've got to—

ALEX: I'll have a think about it, but for now you should back the Soviets.

MARTIN: I think you're wrong. I think they'll—

ALEX: Look, it doesn't matter, do whatever you like, it doesn't matter.

MARTIN: What do you mean it doesn't matter?

ALEX: Listen, I've got to drive all the way to Wodonga—

MARTIN: There's something else.

ALEX: What?

MARTIN *bursts into tears.*

Jesus, Martin… Get a grip of yourself…

ALEX *gives him an awkward hug.*

MARTIN: I'm sorry…

ALEX: Heh, it's all right.

MARTIN: It's just getting too much for me… and Annette's being a pain.

ALEX: Yeah, yeah, keep it down a bit, Martin.

MARTIN: Fucking living this double life, risking all this stuff, everyone thinking I'm a fucking commie, and too gutless to fight in Vietnam… But Annette, oh no, she's not impressed. She's a fucking bitch.

Pause. MARTIN *pulls himself together.*

ALEX: You all right?

MARTIN: Yeah…

ALEX: Now listen…

MARTIN: I feel better just getting it off my chest.

ALEX: Yeah, I know, but listen. I'll come round and see you both.

Pause.

MARTIN: Will yah?

ALEX: Why not? She knows about us.

MARTIN: That'd be fantastic. It's not too risky?

ALEX: Not if we do it right. When I've finished with her, Martin, she'll be impressed with you. She'll be very impressed.

MARTIN *laughs.*

You home on Wednesday night?

MARTIN: No, I've got a sub-committee meeting.

ALEX: Thursday?

MARTIN: Railway fraction. Friday night my mum comes round, but I could get rid of her early.

ALEX: I can come up Friday.

MARTIN: Thanks, Alex.

ALEX: I'll drive past about eight-thirty.

MARTIN: Okay.

ALEX: If it's just you and Annette, leave the car in the garage with the garage door open. If there's a problem, park it in the street, and shut the garage door, all right…?

MARTIN: Yeah.

ALEX: You got it?

MARTIN: All clear, car in the garage, problem, car in the street…

ALEX: Now don't worry so much, you're doing fine, you're a champion.

MARTIN *nods. Pause.*

Are you going?

MARTIN: I was waiting for you to go.

ALEX: I'm staying here. You go, and I'll stay here.

MARTIN: Okay.

ALEX: And then when you've gone, I'll go.

MARTIN: Okay.

> MARTIN *goes.* ALEX *goes.*

◆ ◆ ◆ ◆ ◆

SCENE TWO

TRIXIE *has come around for tea at Martin and Annette's. They've finished eating.* TRIXIE *has drunk quite a bit of beer.*

TRIXIE: Bernard was the older brother. Do you remember your Uncle Bernie?

MARTIN: Yeah. He was all right.

TRIXIE: He was nice enough to you kids, but get some drink in him and he'd turn into a real Jekyll and Hyde… Used to knock his wife around, and she was just a tiny thing, Eileen.

MARTIN: Did he?

TRIXIE: It was a terrible scandal. All the brothers knew about it, but Martin's dad was the only one with the guts to say anything. He fought with Bernie over it, and their mother was so furious she swore she'd never talk to Ron again, and she didn't, not really, not until after Eileen finally left Bernie, and that was the year of the Olympics… 1956.

MARTIN: Mum.

TRIXIE: Come to think of it, it was during the Olympics—

MARTIN: Mum.

TRIXIE: It was the day the Russians played the Hungarians in the water polo, and there was all that blood in the water… That must have made an impression on you, Martin.

> MARTIN *ignores her.*

I never really knew Eileen. Bernie kept her right away from everybody, didn't like her going out. [*Pause.*] And now they're both dead.

MARTIN: Mum, don't you think you should be getting home now?

TRIXIE: I'm all right.

She pours herself a glass of beer, emptying the bottle.

Oh, look what I've gone and done. Poured myself a beer with nary a thought for anyone else, and now the bottle's empty...

She proceeds to pour some of her beer into MARTIN's *and* ANNETTE's *glasses.*

It's share and share alike in your house, isn't it, Martin?

ANNETTE *giggles.*

ANNETTE: There's more beer in the fridge.

MARTIN: She's had enough.

ANNETTE: Oh, come on.

MARTIN: She's not meant to be drinking at all. The doctor warned her.

ANNETTE: You can have mine, Trix, I don't want it.

She pushes her glass over to TRIXIE.

TRIXIE: Oh good, more for the common pool from which everyone can take their share.

TRIXIE *pours the beer from* ANNETTE's *glass into hers.*

MARTIN: It's not funny, Mum. You're not funny.

ANNETTE *is laughing.*

She's not funny! If you really want to talk about the merits of communism, fine, go ahead, we'll discuss it, but there's no need to make fun of something I believe in... So go on... What's your problem with it? What's your problem with communism?

ANNETTE *stares at him.*

That's shut you up, hasn't it?

ANNETTE: You don't have to be rude Martin.

MARTIN: All they want is for people to get a better deal out of life. They want to share the good things around. Is that such a fucking crime?

TRIXIE: I do not wish to discuss it. I know what I think and there's nothing you could say that would change my mind in any way. Communism has stolen you away from me, and from God. It has fouled your language, and in my opinion it's the root of all evil. [*Pause.*] Annette, could you get me my coat.

She stands up.

ANNETTE: Oh no, Trix, sit down.

TRIXIE: I want my coat.

ANNETTE: Come on, sit down. I'll get us another bottle of beer.

She gets up.

MARTIN: There's no more.

ANNETTE: Yes there is

MARTIN: No there's not.

ANNETTE: You didn't even look.

TRIXIE *has got her coat and put it on, and is walking out.*

Martin…

TRIXIE *exits.*

Trix… why did you do that?

MARTIN *checks she's gone.*

MARTIN: Oh, she gives me the shits. She's got no respect for anything I believe in.

ANNETTE: What do you mean, what you believe in?

MARTIN: She makes digs all the time. Little jokes all the time…

ANNETTE: About communism.

MARTIN: Yeah.

ANNETTE: And that upsets you.

MARTIN: Yeah.

ANNETTE: You're perverse, Martin.

MARTIN: I am not.

ANNETTE: Why are you so mean to her? You rub it in, like you want to hurt her.

MARTIN: It's none of your business.

ANNETTE: She thinks it's her fault.

MARTIN: Other people's children become communists, and it doesn't ruin their parents' lives. Jesus.

ANNETTE: Yeah, but you're just pretending you became a communist.

MARTIN: So what's the difference?

ANNETTE: You could tell her, Martin.

MARTIN: I'm not going to tell her. Listen—

ANNETTE: She'd love it, she'd love you being a spy against the communists.

MARTIN: Listen, shut up a minute—

ANNETTE: She wouldn't tell anybody.

MARTIN: Annette, Annette, listen to me. We're going to have a visitor.

ANNETTE: Who?

MARTIN: My controller. He wants to meet you.

ANNETTE: Does he?

MARTIN: I told him all about you, and he wants to meet you.

ANNETTE: Does he want me to be a spy?

MARTIN: No, I don't think so.

ANNETTE: When's he coming?

MARTIN: He's coming really soon. That's why I had to get rid of Mum.

ANNETTE: Oh no, Martin. You should've told me. I'll have to get changed.

> ANNETTE *exits.*

MARTIN: You look fine.

ANNETTE: [*offstage*] Get me the iron.

MARTIN: Where is it?

ANNETTE: [*offstage*] In the cupboard. In the hall cupboard.

> MARTIN *exits.* ANNETTE *re-enters in her petticoat with a dress over her arm.* MARTIN *re-enters with the ironing board. They look at each other.*

MARTIN: I don't think we've got time for the iron... He'll be here any minute.

> *He takes the ironing board off.*

ANNETTE: What does he want to see me for?

MARTIN: [*coming back in*] He just wants to meet you. Put your dress on.

ANNETTE: He won't ask me any questions, will he?

MARTIN: What about?

ANNETTE: Oh, Martin, I'm really nervous.

MARTIN: You'll be all right.

> MARTIN *zips her up. He kisses her on the back of the neck.*

ANNETTE: We've got nothing to give him, no biscuits or anything. You really should've told me.

MARTIN: Give him some of George's olives.

ANNETTE: Communist olives.

MARTIN: We don't have to tell him that.

ANNETTE *goes and gets the olives. They sit down on the couch to wait.*

ANNETTE: What's he like?

MARTIN: He's a nice bloke.

Little pause.

ANNETTE: Do I call him Alex?

MARTIN: Yeah… That's not his real name though…

Little pause.

ANNETTE: Is he married?

MARTIN: His wife left him.

Pause. A knock at the door. ANNETTE *is containing her excitement.* MARTIN *opens the door.* FRANK *enters.*

Frank.

FRANK: Yeah. We tried to ring you.

MARTIN: What is it?

FRANK: No one could get through.

MARTIN: Aaah, the phone's off the hook.

He rights it. PHYLLIS *enters.*

FRANK: Phyll's been trying for last couple of hours. To tell you about the meeting.

MARTIN: What meeting?

FRANK: We called an extraordinary meeting. We wanted to respond straight away. But we haven't got a quorum, so we all hopped in the Valiant. Lucky you're home.

ELLI *and* GEORGE *enter.*

MARTIN: But what's happened?

PHYLLIS: Russia's invaded Czechoslovakia.

MARTIN: Oh, God…

FRANK: They didn't invade, Phyllis. Can you stop using the word invade. There's no need to inflame the situation further.

PHYLLIS: They did invade.

GEORGE *turns on the TV and finds a news report. Shouting, sirens, shooting sounds.*

FRANK: They didn't. They were invited to come in.

GEORGE: Who invited them?

FRANK: A group in the Czech government.

PHYLLIS: Oh, bullshit.

MARTIN: Annette, maybe you'd better—

PHYLLIS: They drove their tanks down the streets of Prague. It was on the television.

> PHYLLIS *tries not to cry.* ELLI *comforts her. They all watch the TV for a moment.*

ANNETTE: But… aren't they on the same side?

ELLI: That's what we all thought.

> PHYLLIS *sees the olives and clocks the dress.*

PHYLLIS: I hope you didn't have anything planned.

MARTIN: No, no… we just had Mum round.

FRANK: I'm sorry about this, Annette. I'm sorry to land on you unannounced.

ANNETTE: That's all right.

FRANK: But we should start…

> *Pause.*

ANNETTE: Would anyone like a cup of tea?

> *Everyone shakes their head. They are all at a bit of a loss.*

PHYLLIS: I can't believe it. I still can't believe it. I thought they'd worked it all out at Bratislava, that's what they said…

FRANK: Calm down a bit, Phyllis.

PHYLLIS: Oh, I don't want to listen to you.

FRANK: Let's start the bloody meeting… Martin…

MARTIN: I'm just going to move the car.

ANNETTE: Move it where? It's in the garage.

MARTIN: Yeah, I know.

> *Pause. Everyone looks at him.*

I don't want it in the garage… I want it in the street… [*Pause.*] I thought we could have the meeting in the garage.

FRANK: In the garage…?

MARTIN: Yeah…

PHYLLIS: We're fine here, Martin. We're fine.

ANNETTE: There's nothing for you to sit on in the garage.

MARTIN *gives her a dirty look.*

MARTIN: We can take our chairs in there. I think it's best. [*Pause.*] So I'll just move the car.

He exits. They look after him, perplexed. He quickly re-enters.

Aah, Frank... the Valiant's blocking the driveway...

FRANK *and* MARTIN *exit.* ANNETTE *exits. The others all pick up chairs and exit.*

◆ ◆ ◆ ◆ ◆

SCENE THREE

The Communist Party members are sitting on their chairs in the garage. An unshielded single light bulb hangs down. They are depressed and are just sitting there waiting for FRANK *who is scribbling.*

PHYLLIS: Are you ready, Frank?

Pause. FRANK *rubs something out and scribbles some more... there is another pause. The rest of them sit there, lost in misery.*

FRANK: Okay...

Everyone looks up reluctantly.

I move that we send a motion of censure to the National Executive in Sydney, for taking precipitate action in officially criticising the Soviet Union and their allies for their actions in Czechoslovakia, without consulting the Party, that on an issue like this there should be due democratic process—

JEAN *enters and takes her seat.*

JEAN: I'm sorry I'm late.

FRANK *passes the motion to* PHYLLIS.

FRANK: Pass that to Jean.

PHYLLIS: Is there a seconder for this motion?

MARTIN *puts up his hand. Everyone looks at him.* ELLI *gasps.*

All those in favour?

FRANK *and a hesitant* MARTIN *put up their hands.*

All those against?

ELLI, GEORGE, PHYLLIS *and* JEAN *put up their hands.*

Motion defeated... Is that it, Frank?

FRANK: No. I've got another one. I move that the Australian Communist Party should immediately apologise to the Communist Party of the Soviet Union, and acknowledge that they are living in Europe and are in a better position than us to know what is going on there, and judge the dangers of the situation accordingly.

PHYLLIS: Is there a seconder for this motion?

MARTIN *puts up his hand.*

All those in favour?

FRANK *and* MARTIN *put up their hands.*

All those against?

ELLI, GEORGE, PHYLLIS *and* JEAN *put up their hands.*

Motion defeated.

FRANK *slumps back in his chair.*

ELLI: I have a motion. I move that the South Bendigo Branch of the Communist Party of Australia heartily endorse the actions of the National Executive over the recent crisis in Czechoslovakia, and deplore the actions of the Soviet Union and three other socialist countries in occupying Czechoslovakia. We call for the withdrawal of the occupation troops, respect for the Bratislava Agreement, recognition of the elected leadership of the Czechoslovak government and Party, and respect for their liberty and persons.

PHYLLIS: Is there a seconder for this motion?

GEORGE *puts up his hand.*

All those in favour?

ELLI, GEORGE, PHYLLIS *and* JEAN *put up their hands.*

All those against?

FRANK *and* MARTIN *put up their hands.*

Motion carried.

They sit in miserable silence.

◆ ◆ ◆ ◆ ◆

SCENE FOUR

ALEX *and* MARTIN *are in Martin's garage, much later that night. They're drinking scotch, and are a bit pissed.*

MARTIN: It felt like an age, you know, it felt like hours, and then, from out of somewhere in my head, somewhere deep down, came this voice, I didn't consciously think of it, you know…

ALEX: Yeah, that's magnificent. You've really taken it into your body…

MARTIN: Yeah.

ALEX: It's become a reflex.

MARTIN: Yeah.

ALEX: That's what you got to do.

MARTIN: But, oh fuck, I was so fucking nervous that you'd just walk in and we'd all be standing in the fucking living room together, the spies and the commies all together in the fucking living room, just looking at each other, the world blown into pieces, you know. Oh, man, what a trip, what a fucking trip…

> *They laugh. They swig the whisky.*

And somewhere in my head I was going over what you said the other morning and I realised what you meant.

> *Pause.*

ALEX: What?

MARTIN: You get it all first, don't you… way before the papers. You could've told me, I wouldn't have told anybody, honestly Alex, you can trust me.

ALEX: What are you talking about?

MARTIN: Russia invading Czechoslovakia.

ALEX: No, I didn't know.

MARTIN: You didn't?

ALEX: Nuh.

MARTIN: Oh.

ALEX: Sorry.

> *Pause.*

MARTIN: But I thought… when you said…

ALEX: Martin, you know there's things I can't tell you.

MARTIN: Yeah, I know.

ALEX: That's just the way it is.

MARTIN: Yeah, that's all right... [*Pause.*] You know the Party's come out very strongly against the Soviet Union.

ALEX: Yeah, I know.

MARTIN: So, what... you think they'll knuckle back under or...?

ALEX: Stop digging, Martin.

MARTIN: I wasn't...

ALEX: It'd be putting my head on a block to tell you about it. [*Pause.*] Have you ever heard of James Jesus Angleton?

MARTIN: No.

ALEX: No, you wouldn't have.

MARTIN: Who is he?

ALEX: He's the Head of Counter Espionage in the CIA.

MARTIN: You met him?

ALEX: I took him flying.

MARTIN: Yeah?

ALEX: I own a Piper Cherokee.

MARTIN: Wow.

ALEX: Yeah.

MARTIN: How come they let you?

ALEX: Let me what?

MARTIN: Let you take him flying. If he's the Head of the CIA.

ALEX: He's not the Head of the CIA, he's the Head of Counter Espionage. He's the real thing, Martin. He runs spies around the world.

MARTIN: What was he doing in Australia?

ALEX: You better be right that you don't open your mouth about this. This is so fucking secret. No one knows this. No one. I just know 'cause I own a plane, and they wanted someone they could trust to fly them to Coober Pedy.

MARTIN: Them?

ALEX: Yeah... he came with a friend.

MARTIN: Who?

ALEX: Jim called him Anatole, I don't know if that's his real name but he's the most important defector that America's ever had. Fucking so high up in the KGB, a commander or something, gave them spies and counter-spies on plates. In the early sixties they were falling like ninepins.

MARTIN: Fuck.

ALEX: They loved it here. They loved Australia. Jim said it reminded him of Mexico… Anyway this guy, Anatole, he likes to talk, so does Jim, funny eh, but maybe they thought they were miles away from anywhere, or maybe they just liked me, I dunno, but a thousand miles above the Little Desert, they told me stuff that just blew my mind, and it's been burning a hole in my head ever since, fucking almost sent me crazy… They're so smart the Russians, they're so fucking smart… When Anatole defects, right, to the Americans, they check him out, they spend months talking to them, 'cause he's a big fish, and they want to know if he's the genuine article, and he checks out, everything he says checks out, and then he tells them that he was part of this fancy think-tank, a sort of KGB inside the KGB, and that the KGB we know about is a sort of front, a fake, and there's a real KGB that's so hidden away that we've never heard of it, until he arrives, and tells them about it, and the stuff they do, fuck…

MARTIN: The real KGB.

ALEX: Yeah.

MARTIN: What. What do they do?

ALEX: You swear you won't tell a living soul.

> MARTIN *nods.*

Russia's just driven their tanks through Prague. It's all there in the papers.

MARTIN: Yeah.

ALEX: Old-style communism versus new Euro communism and the rest of it. The countries behind the Iron Curtain in disarray.

MARTIN: Yeah.

ALEX: It's all bullshit, it's all orchestrated, there's no divisions, no arguments, it's the biggest con job the world has ever seen.

MARTIN: What?!

ALEX: It's incredible, isn't it?

MARTIN: I don't understand.

ALEX: There is no division between any of the communist states. It's a huge manufactured diversion so the West get gleeful about the rifts, and stop watching the ball.

MARTIN: Oh, my God.

ALEX: Hungary was all crap, never happened, the China Soviet split, all made up, never happened…

MARTIN: No…

ALEX: And now Czechoslovakia, total invention…

MARTIN: But did the tanks really roll—?

ALEX: Yeah, of course the tanks rolled down the street, but then they get out and they go inside and drink vodka together, and have a good laugh.

MARTIN: Is that true?

ALEX: That's what the Americans told me.

MARTIN: Fuck… Does Frank know?

◆ ◆ ◆ ◆ ◆

SCENE FIVE

GEORGE *is sitting at home. There is a knock at the door.* ALEX *and his offsider,* VINCENT, *enter, with a* POLICEWOMAN.

VINCENT: [*mispronouncing*] Mr Tassakis.

GEORGE: Tassakis.

VINCENT: We're from the Department of Immigration.

GEORGE: Oh, yeah.

ALEX: Do you have electricity here?

GEORGE: Sorry?

ALEX: Electricity. Do you have electricity?

GEORGE: Yes I've got electricity.

ALEX: I'd like to plug in my tape recorder and record our conversation.

GEORGE: Why do you want to tape it?

ALEX: So we have a record of interview.

GEORGE: Who are you exactly?

VINCENT: We're from the Department of Immigration, Mr Tassakis.

GEORGE: From Melbourne? I sent my forms to Melbourne.

VINCENT: Yeah, we got your forms.

GEORGE: Why have you come all this way to interview me?

ALEX: You applied to be naturalised.

GEORGE: Surely you don't interview everybody?

ALEX: Everybody has an interview, Mr Tassakis.

GEORGE: It's Tassakis. I'm from Criti. It's Tassakis.

ALEX: Are you willing to answer some questions?

GEORGE: I want to see identification.

VINCENT: You've got very good English, haven't you? Very good.

GEORGE: You want me to speak in Greek?

VINCENT: No, I just wondered why you speak English so well.

GEORGE: I speak five languages.

VINCENT: Five, that's a lot, isn't it? Do you speak Russian? Is Russian one of them?

GEORGE: No. Why is the police here?

ALEX: To make you feel more comfortable.

GEORGE: Have I committed a crime? What is this?

ALEX: We're just asking you a few questions.

GEORGE: What is this? What is this?

ALEX: Sit down, please.

GEORGE: I don't want to sit down.

ALEX: Sit down.

GEORGE: No, I'm not going to sit down.

VINCENT: Sit down.

GEORGE: You can't make me.

ALEX: Mr Tassakis… you're making this very hard.

      GEORGE *walks over to the window.*

GEORGE: I will stand here and you can ask me your questions.

VINCENT: Why do you want to stand there?

GEORGE: It's next to the window.

VINCENT: What's out the window?

GEORGE: There's nothing out the window.

      ALEX *looks at the* POLICEWOMAN. *The* POLICEWOMAN *goes and peers out the window. She turns around and shakes her head.*

ALEX: All right, Mr Tassakis. We'll bring a chair over and you can sit down.

      ALEX *nods at* VINCENT *to take him a chair.*

Sit down, please.

      GEORGE *doesn't.* VINCENT *pushes the chair into his legs.*

Sit down, please.

GEORGE *has no choice but to sit.*

VINCENT: What do you think of the Berlin Wall?

GEORGE: What?

VINCENT: The Berlin Wall, what do you think of it?

GEORGE: I've not seen it.

VINCENT: You think it's a good idea, a big wall like that?

GEORGE: I dunno.

VINCENT: Keep all the commies from running away...

GEORGE *shrugs.*

If people try and cross over, they get shot, and hang bleeding and squealing on the barbed wire. Do you like that idea?

GEORGE: Not particularly.

VINCENT: Do you think we should have a wall like that?

GEORGE: No... Where?

VINCENT: Around Australia.

GEORGE: Around the coast?

VINCENT: What do you think of that idea?

GEORGE: I think that's a stupid idea.

VINCENT: So you don't want a wall... What about a curtain?

GEORGE *stands up.*

GEORGE: You're wasting my time. I think you'd—

ALEX: Sit down, Mr Tassakis.

GEORGE *reluctantly sits back down.* ALEX *nods to* VINCENT.

VINCENT: Let's talk about your kids... Calliope and Christos. Have I the right pronunciation?

GEORGE *ignores him.*

Do they go to church?

GEORGE: They sometimes go to church.

VINCENT: How often would you say?

GEORGE: Easter... Christmas...

VINCENT: You let them go to church.

GEORGE: I let them go.

VINCENT: But you're a communist, aren't you, Mr Tassakis?

GEORGE: No, I'm not a communist.

VINCENT: So where would I have got that idea?

GEORGE: I don't know…

ALEX: Were you ever a communist?

GEORGE: No.

ALEX: Do you ever attend meetings of the Communist Party?

GEORGE: No.

ALEX: Do you ever have meetings of the Communist Party in your house?

GEORGE: No.

ALEX: I think you're lying, Mr Tassakis.

GEORGE: No.

VINCENT: What's your opinion of Red China?

GEORGE: I think they've gone astray.

ALEX: And Soviet Russia?

GEORGE: A great experiment perhaps, but a sad failure.

ALEX: I think you are a communist, Mr Tassakis.

GEORGE: No. You've got me mistaken. I'm a small businessman. I vote for Mr Gorton.

VINCENT: Don't bullshit / me.

GEORGE: [*to the* POLICEWOMAN] Are they allowed to ask me these questions?

POLICEWOMAN: Yes / they are, sir.

VINCENT: You're a liar. You're a dirty, little, commie, Greek bastard.

> GEORGE *swears at him angrily in Greek.*

GEORGE: [*in Greek*] Get fucked, you wanker, you donkey, you make me sick to my stomach.

VINCENT: Don't threaten me, mate—

GEORGE: [*in Greek*] You're a stupid child. You have no humanity.

ALEX: We'd like to see inside your shop now.

> GEORGE *is still angry, but he bites his tongue.*

GEORGE: It's all put away. It's all shut away.

ALEX: You can open it, can't you?

GEORGE: No I can't. My wife has the key.

ALEX: That would be Elena… [*giving her surname a peculiar emphasis*] … Tassakis. [*Pause.*] Is that right, George?

GEORGE: That's right.

VINCENT: What's your cousin's name, George?

GEORGE: I have a lot of cousins.

VINCENT: The one that went to America.

GEORGE: I'm not sure to who you're referring.

VINCENT: He lives in Baltimore.

GEORGE: Well, you sound like you know already.

VINCENT: You tell us.

GEORGE: His name is George Tassakis.

ALEX: But that's your name.

GEORGE: We have the same name.

ALEX: Aah… Well, that clears things up a bit.

VINCENT: Yeah, that clears things up a bit.

> *Pause.*

ALEX: So who's George Zannos?

◆ ◆ ◆ ◆ ◆

SCENE SIX

ELLI *is at the police station. The* POLICEWOMAN *enters.*

POLICEWOMAN: Mrs Tassakis.

> ELLI *stands up.*

I'm afraid you won't be able to see him today.

ELLI: Why not?

POLICEWOMAN: The Embassy people are with him.

ELLI: What Embassy people?

POLICEWOMAN: People from the Greek Embassy. They flew down from Canberra.

ELLI: Well, I'll wait till they've gone.

POLICEWOMAN: No I'm sorry, Mrs Tassakis. It won't be possible today.

ELLI: This is bullshit. I'm allowed to see him.

POLICEWOMAN: Why don't you come back tomorrow?

ELLI: You go and get your superior.

POLICEWOMAN: Mrs Tassakis—

ELLI: I've got a lawyer coming here in half an hour who is going to want to see my husband. Are you going to say he can't see him? Can't see his wife. Can't see his lawyer. You call yourself a democracy!

POLICEWOMAN: I'll go and check again. Sit down, please.

> *The* POLICEWOMAN *exits.* MARTIN *enters.*

MARTIN: Frank can't find the lawyer. But he says there's a bloke in Ballarat that might be okay. And that'd be quicker.

ELLI: [*in Greek*] Mary, our Mother—

MARTIN: It'll be all right.

The POLICEWOMAN *re-enters.*

POLICEWOMAN: You can see him.

ELLI *pulls herself together.*

You'll have to wait, though. Go through there, and talk to the officer on the desk. He'll show you where to sit.

ELLI: You go home, Martin.

MARTIN: Are you sure? I can wait for you.

ELLI: Come round later.

MARTIN *kisses her on the cheek.*

Thank you.

ELLI *exits. The* POLICEWOMAN *gives* MARTIN *a curious glance as he turns to go.*

MARTIN: What are you looking at?

POLICEWOMAN: I remember you. From school. You played football with my brother…

MARTIN: Oh, yeah.

POLICEWOMAN: Craig Ingram.

MARTIN: Oh, yeah.

POLICEWOMAN: He said you'd turned out really weird…

MARTIN *says nothing.*

You protest against the war and stuff, don't you?

MARTIN: Just fuck off.

He leaves.

◆ ◆ ◆ ◆ ◆

SCENE SEVEN

MARTIN *is on the phone at his house. It is afternoon, but quite dark in the room as all the blinds are pulled down.*

MARTIN: [*on the phone*] ASIO. [*Pause. He spells it out.*] A.S.I.O. [*Pause.*] Australian Security… Organisation… Oh look, I don't know what the 'I' stands for… Does it matter? Can't you look under the initials?… Jesus Christ, this is really important. This is a matter of national security… Intelligence. Australian Security Intelligence Organisation… Thank *you*… [*Pause.*] You must have a listing… No, you must… [*Pause.*] Of course it fucking exists. Of course it fucking exists.

They hang up on him. He slams the phone down. ANNETTE *enters.*

ANNETTE: What's wrong?

MARTIN *says nothing.*

Martin?

He ignores her.

What's it so dark in here for?

She pulls up the blinds and light streams in. MARTIN *jumps up.*

MARTIN: No, I want them down.

He pulls the blinds down again. Pause.

ANNETTE: What's happened?

MARTIN: Nothing's happened.

ANNETTE: Martin…

MARTIN: I think… my cover might be in danger.

ANNETTE: What do you mean?

MARTIN: I think the Party could find out about me.

ANNETTE: How come?

MARTIN: It's too hard to explain.

ANNETTE: What's happened?

MARTIN: George has been arrested.

ANNETTE: For being a communist?

MARTIN: No, no, not for being a communist. That's not illegal.

ANNETTE: What for then?

MARTIN: I don't know what for.

ANNETTE: Well, what's it got to do with you?

MARTIN: It could just point to me. That's all. All right?

ANNETTE: What's going on, Martin? What have you done?

MARTIN: Nothing. I haven't done anything. Fucking hell. I'm not the criminal here.

ANNETTE: No, George is apparently.

MARTIN: You know nothing about George. You know nothing about him. So keep your big mouth shut. [*Pause.*] Look, I didn't mean that. I'm sorry. [*Pause.*] I'm under pressure…
ANNETTE: Is George some sort of… saboteur?

> MARTIN *has got slightly frenzied and very aggressive.*

MARTIN: Fucking shut up, Annette. I don't want to talk about it.

> *Pause.* ANNETTE *picks up her keys and walks out of the house.*

◆ ◆ ◆ ◆ ◆

SCENE EIGHT

That night, MARTIN *and* ELLI *are at Elli's house sipping raki. The mood is sad and sombre.*

ELLI: Ten years we've been here. More than ten. In Melbourne first… and then here… Christos was born here… [*Pause.*] What's the time?
MARTIN: Quarter to one.
ELLI: You should go home, Martin.

> MARTIN *doesn't move.*

I didn't think this week could get any worse, after… But things can always get worse… [*In Greek*] My heart is bleeding. It was on a day like this that I lost my heart. My heart is bleeding. [*Pause.*] Why did you change your mind?
MARTIN: Me?
ELLI: And vote with Frank. I thought you were excited by the New Communism.
MARTIN: I was, but—
ELLI: I couldn't believe it. George and I haven't known what to say to you.
MARTIN: I thought… I thought, maybe there was a threat from West Germany.
ELLI: I don't think so.
MARTIN: It all happened so quickly… I had hardly any time to think about it.
ELLI: What was there to think about?

> MARTIN *pulls out a packet of cigarettes.*

When did you start smoking?

MARTIN *stuffs them back in his pocket.*

MARTIN: Oh… I don't really… just occasionally… [*Pause.*] I suppose I thought, with the stakes as high as the long-term survival of communism, it was better to take… the cautious road.

ELLI: But you can't think one thing one day, think it passionately, and then the next day, think the complete opposite. [*Pause.*] Does any of this really matter to you, Martin?

MARTIN: Yes.

ELLI: Why? What matters?

Pause.

MARTIN: You matter to me.

Pause.

ELLI: Frank's never really trusted you. Did you know that?

MARTIN: No.

ELLI: He wanted to check up on you, after you joined, but George and I told him he was a suspicious old man, and if you can't trust a young working-class boy, a beautiful boy, who came to communism like a duck in water, then who can you trust?

MARTIN *doesn't move.* ELLI *cries.*

I hate him being in there… in that little room.

MARTIN: It'll be all right.

ELLI: Have you ever been in prison?

MARTIN: No.

ELLI: He's nearly fifty. He shouldn't have to sit in that stupid little room all by himself… You should go home. It's late. [*Pause.*] Go on. Go home, Martin.

Pause. MARTIN *is very moved. It looks like he is going to confess.*

MARTIN: I'm so sorry…

ELLI: What for?

Pause.

MARTIN: I voted the wrong way about Czechoslovakia.

ELLI: Don't worry about it. [*Pause.*] The whole world seems without hope, the right are hypocrites, and the left is poisoned, there's no unity in the socialist world, where there should be, we fight and fight amongst ourselves, there's no unity…

She is very sad.

MARTIN: It'll be all right.

ELLI: No it won't.

　　　MARTIN *hugs her. After a few moments he tries to kiss her.*

[*Pushing him away*] What are you doing?

MARTIN: I don't know what I'm doing... I'm sorry... I should go...

　　　He makes to go.

ELLI: Martin... Do you remember one night, you hadn't been in the Party long, you and me and George were drinking, and we were talking.

MARTIN: Which particular night?

ELLI: We were talking about Greece, and I told you about George, about his history... his political history...

MARTIN: Sort of... that's three years ago...

ELLI: You didn't tell anybody, did you?

MARTIN: No... no... I hardly even remember... I must have been so drunk.

ELLI: You didn't tell Annette.

MARTIN: No, no, I don't tell her anything. I don't tell her any of the Party stuff...

ELLI: They know about George.

MARTIN: What do they know?

ELLI: They know his real name. If they send him back to Greece now, he'll go straight to jail. They'll murder him. The colonels are ruthless. There are terrible stories.

MARTIN: Oh, Elli...

ELLI: You didn't tell anybody? Anybody at all?

MARTIN: No...

　　　They stare at each other.

I can't remember much of that night... the music and the raki, whatever it was... I went home and slept like a log...

ELLI: Frank knows, but I can't see him telling anyone, and my cousin knows, maybe she said something, but it seems unlikely...

MARTIN: Maybe something happened in Greece...

ELLI: Maybe.

　　　They stare at each other.

MARTIN: I didn't tell anybody. I wouldn't do a thing like that. Jesus, Elli.

　　　Pause.

ELLI: I'll see you tomorrow. At the meeting.

MARTIN *nods. He gets up awkwardly.*

◆ ◆ ◆ ◆ ◆

SCENE NINE

Later that night. MARTIN *is sitting in his room at his tape recorder, off his face with fear. He presses record.*

MARTIN: George Tassakis has been arrested and interrogated on the charge of having a false name on his passport. They've refused bail. The Greek Embassy are involved somehow… but then you'd know that, wouldn't you…? Frank Nash says that… Oh, fucking hell, fucking hell, why didn't anyone fucking tell me about this. They know about me. I can't fucking do this, they fucking know about me. Where are you? I left all the blinds pulled down, and no one came. I waited for two hours in the fucking park, and no one came… Then I had to go and see Elena Tassakis, 'cause I said I would, and she knows about me, she fucking knows about me… The meeting's tomorrow. I've got to talk to you before the meeting. What do I do? Do I just fuck off out of here? Why didn't anyone tell me you were going to do this? Jesus. What if they're fucking following me? How'm I going to do this drop? What if they see me?

He presses stop. He presses re-wind. He tries to pull himself together. He lights a cigarette. He presses record.

ANNETTE: [*offstage*] Martin.

MARTIN: Go away.

ANNETTE enters.

What are you doing back here?

ANNETTE: Trixie's had a stroke. I've been at the hospital. They couldn't find you, so they called me at Mum's.

Pause.

MARTIN: Annette, I'm in such fucking trouble.

ANNETTE: I don't want to hear about it.

◆ ◆ ◆ ◆ ◆

Above: Tom Long as Martin; below: Tom Long as Martin and Kerry Walker as Trixie in the 2004 Company B production. (Photos: Heidrun Löhr)

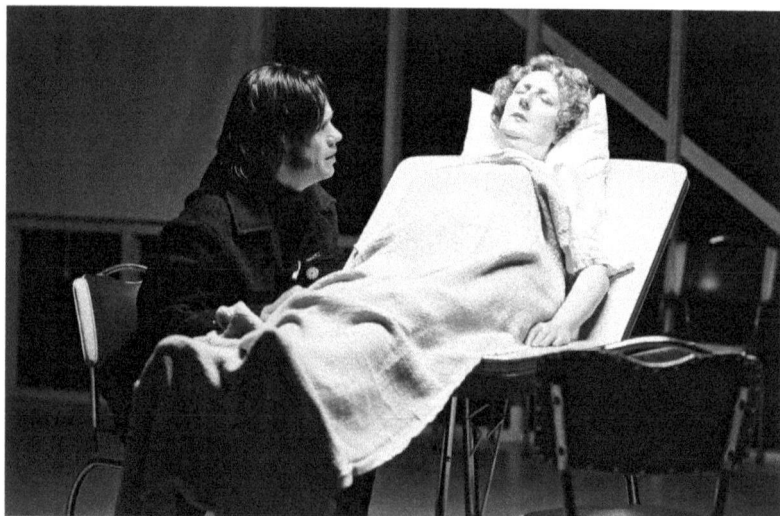

SCENE TEN

TRIXIE *is propped in her hospital bed.* MARTIN *sits next to her.*

TRIXIE: Peter.
MARTIN: It's Martin, Mum.
TRIXIE: Martin. Get us a drink will you, a drink of water.
MARTIN: I don't think you're allowed, Mum... [*Pause.*] Mum, I've got
    something I have to tell you.
TRIXIE: I know what you're going to say.
MARTIN: Do you?
TRIXIE: I worked it out myself. No help from you...

      MARTIN *is a bit taken aback.*

Do you think you could keep something like that from me?
MARTIN: I would've told you. I wasn't allowed to tell you.
TRIXIE: Yeah, well I've known for ages... All those silly lies.
MARTIN: Yeah?
TRIXIE: I knew there had to be something more to it.
MARTIN: Oh, Mum, I'm sorry.
TRIXIE: You're going to marry that Maori girl.
MARTIN: No—
TRIXIE: You're going to marry an Islander girl. [*She laughs.*] I was
    shocked at first... Mum's going to hang, draw and quarter you.
MARTIN: That's Peter, Mum. That's your brother Peter. He's dead. He
    died in New Zealand. I'm Martin. Your son Martin.
TRIXIE: Martin. Martin.
MARTIN: Mum, something bad's happened to me. Something really bad.
TRIXIE: What's happened?

      MARTIN *is silent, thinking how to put it into words.*

Is it my fault?
MARTIN: No. I don't know whose fault it is... but I think I've done
    something really bad.
TRIXIE: Go to church, love. That's what it's there for.

      Pause. MARTIN *talks very quietly.*

MARTIN: It was a few years ago, and I'd only just started working for—

TRIXIE: What are you whispering for? I can't hear you.

> MARTIN *quickly glances around the ward. It's hard to break the pattern of secrecy.*

MARTIN: Listen, Mum, I was very young, and keen, you know…? And I've been thinking a lot about it—

TRIXIE: That's good, love. Thinking's good. But talk a bit louder, will you?

MARTIN: And I've been wondering if I found out now what I found out then, whether I'd tell them, or whether I'd just keep it to myself, weigh up the consequences, and make a personal decision, and keep it to myself. Or whether, even now, I would tell them, because I'd feel like I had to tell them.

TRIXIE: Hold my hand.

> MARTIN *takes her hand.*

MARTIN: I'd like to think I wouldn't tell them. [*He pauses again.*] I didn't realise what it meant, Mum.

TRIXIE: You may as well be talking Greek, darl, I don't know what you're saying.

MARTIN: I'm a spy, Mum. I'm a dirty rotten spy.

> TRIXIE *shuts her eyes.*

TRIXIE: I'm just going to shut my eyes for a moment, Peter.

MARTIN: I'm not Peter. I'm Martin. I'm your son Martin.

TRIXIE: You're obviously very distressed, whoever you are…

> MARTIN *sits holding* TRIXIE*'s hand.* TRIXIE *keeps breathing, just.*

◆ ◆ ◆ ◆ ◆

SCENE ELEVEN

FRANK *and* JEAN *are at Frank's house, waiting for the meeting. They're muttering softly together.*

FRANK: I dunno what the correct procedure is.

JEAN: No.

FRANK: I'm going to have to tell them, though. They'll send someone down.

MARTIN *enters. They stop talking and look at him. No one says anything for a moment.*

MARTIN: Where is everyone? [*Pause.*] Where's Elli?

FRANK: She's gone. They flew them back to Greece this morning.

MARTIN: What?!

FRANK: Both of them.

MARTIN: But I—

FRANK: They picked her up and took her away. Didn't even let her pack. Left all their stuff in the house. They've ransacked the place. They've ripped it to shreds, the bastards... [*pause*] ... and they've kept the kids here...

MARTIN: Augh, no...

FRANK: For their own good, they reckon...

MARTIN: Augh, no... Where are they?

FRANK: Some family's looking after them. Someone from the Lions Club or something, I dunno. They wouldn't tell me...

MARTIN: What are we going to do?

FRANK: I was on the phone all morning. The Party'll make a fuss about it. A bloke from the *Tribune*'s coming down to talk to us. And it'll get in the straight press for sure. It's a big story... but I don't know in the end if there's anything we can do. You see... [*looking at* MARTIN] ... George was on a false passport... he was here under a false name.

Pause.

MARTIN: Yeah... I knew that...

Pause.

FRANK: And with that being the case, it's not a civil rights matter, it's a legal one, and Australia has every right to kick him out.

MARTIN: But what about Elli? What about the kids?

FRANK: Elli was on the same passport. We can challenge it, I s'pose. And the kids, they're saying they're in moral danger.

JEAN: From the communists.

MARTIN: You're kidding.

Pause.

JEAN: You look terrible, Martin.

Pause.

MARTIN: Did you get a chance to talk to Elli, before she left. Did you get to say goodbye?

FRANK: Yeah. I talked to her. [*He looks at* MARTIN.] Sit down, Martin.

MARTIN: Oh, look… I gotta go… I'm sorry—

FRANK: Sit down.

MARTIN: No, my mum, my mum's in hospital, she's—

FRANK: I'm sorry about your mother, but this can't wait.

> MARTIN *sits down. They both stare at him.*

We have to take care of our own people. We have to make sure there are no breaches of discipline, nothing that can bring the Party into disrepute, let alone harbour people actively working against the Party's interests.

> *Pause.* MARTIN *says nothing, just waits for the blow to fall.*

Have you ever heard of the Control Commission?

MARTIN: No.

FRANK: No, it's not much talked about. It's a disciplinary body within the Communist Party. It takes care of security. And matters of disloyalty… treachery…

> *Pause.*

MARTIN: Where's Phyll?

> JEAN *tries not to cry.*

What?

FRANK: She's gone. I told her to fuck off out of here.

MARTIN: What?

FRANK: She's… she's a mole, Martin. I haven't told the Party yet…

MARTIN: No.

FRANK: She is. She's been fucking spying on me since I met her in Horsham.

MARTIN: No, not Phyll… she's not a spy.

FRANK: I know. I couldn't believe it either. She denied it. She swore black and blue that she's not. She swore on her mother's grave that she's not. But she's lying, she's fucking lying. She's a fucking spy.

JEAN: She is, Martin.

FRANK: That big performance over Czechoslovakia, all fucking bullshit.

MARTIN: Phyllis.

FRANK: I don't know if they planted her on me, or if they got to her somehow…

MARTIN: How did you find out?

JEAN: I found out. Phyll asked me if I'd go through some figures with her, so I went round to my sister's. Phyll rents a room there to do her paperwork. She was late, but I've got a key, so I let myself in. And she just didn't come, for ages, and I thought I may as well get some work done before she got there. I wasn't snooping… but inside a drawer in her bureau, I found all this stuff, descriptions of meetings, descriptions of people, who said what when, about all of us, nasty little comments about all of us, and it was in Phyll's handwriting.

MARTIN: Oh, fuck. [*Pause.*] Frank… didn't you meet her in Bathurst?

FRANK: What?

MARTIN: Phyll. I thought you met her in Bathurst.

FRANK: Who told you that?

MARTIN: I dunno, I—

FRANK: I met her in Horsham. She worked at the hospital. She was a nurses' aid.

MARTIN: I thought she was a primary school teacher.

FRANK: Jesus, Martin, what does it matter? She's a fucking spook. And the worst thing is… Phyll knew about George's passport… [*almost in tears*] … because I told her…

> *Pause.*

MARTIN: Did you… tell Elli…?

> FRANK *nods. He can't talk. He puts his head in his hands.* JEAN *puts her arm around him.*

◆ ◆ ◆ ◆ ◆

SCENE TWELVE

A few weeks later. ALEX *and* MARTIN *are meeting at the football ground.* MARTIN *is extremely depressed.*

MARTIN: I want to stop.

ALEX: But you're doing so well.

MARTIN: I want to stop now.

ALEX: But, Marty, you've single-handedly destroyed almost the entire South Bendigo Branch of the Communist Party. They'll take years to re-build. You're a fucking hero.

   MARTIN *says nothing.*

Hey.

   He punches him on the arm. MARTIN *shrugs away irritably.*

You'll be all right… Your mother's just died. It's a hard time. [*Pause.*] How's Annette?

MARTIN: She's moved back with her parents.

ALEX: Oh, that's no good.

MARTIN: You deserted me. You didn't warn me any of that crap was going to happen.

ALEX: I couldn't tell you.

MARTIN: Bullshit.

ALEX: I couldn't.

MARTIN: And why did you have to deport them? Why did you—?

ALEX: Oh, Jesus, Martin. You're turning into a real fucking bleeding heart, you know that? You got too close to them. You got too fucking close to the Greeks. And it's a lesson for you. You wanted to get into her pants, didn't you, Martin? That's why your marriage has broken down, not because you're working for us.

MARTIN: You lied to me. All that stuff about Frank, that was all lies.

ALEX: It was not lies. Jesus, what are you talking about?

MARTIN: He never lived in Bathurst.

ALEX: Well, I was wrong. I'm sorry. It's fucking hard getting accurate information. Christ, I thought you'd be pleased.

MARTIN: Well, I'm not.

ALEX: We got you off the hook. You're as clean as a whistle.

MARTIN: Oh yeah, that's great, isn't it, and what's going to happen to Phyll?

ALEX: Phyll?

MARTIN: Phyll. Frank's girlfriend. The Membership Secretary.

ALEX: Oh, her… She'll be all right. Jesus, I did her a favour, I got her out of the Communist Party.

MARTIN: But she liked being in the Communist Party.

ALEX: Listen to yourself, Martin.

MARTIN: You've fucked up her whole life, Alex… you've… broken up her relationship.

ALEX: Wait a minute. You told me Frank's been having it off with the librarian for the past six months.

MARTIN *says nothing.*

I thought you'd get a kick out of it. I put a lot of work into that. It was a two-man operation, Martin, what with lifting the key, and keeping Phyll busy at the bank, and someone to plant the stuff. I used some of your notes, some very juicy stuff, all copied out in her handwriting.

Pause.

MARTIN: How many of us have you got, Alex?

ALEX: What do you mean?

MARTIN: How many like me?

ALEX: That's confidential, Martin.

MARTIN: Come on, Alex. Like you haven't told me secrets before. Thirty, thirty-five…

ALEX: Something like that…

MARTIN *says nothing.*

Look it's a hard job, Martin, I told you that right from the beginning.

MARTIN: I want to meet some of them.

ALEX: Don't be stupid.

MARTIN: Are they all young men like me?

ALEX: We've got all sorts, men and women. People like confiding in women. They excel at entrapment.

MARTIN: Good for them.

ALEX: Mate…

MARTIN: What?

ALEX: You gotta relax a bit… Do you want a new Party?

MARTIN: What do you mean a new Party?

ALEX: We could put you in the MLs. We're very interested in them.

MARTIN: The Maoists…

ALEX: Yeah.

MARTIN: You got to be kidding.

ALEX: They've got a cell in Bendigo. They're much more covert than the CPA. It'd be a challenge. It's hard getting people in there.

MARTIN: They're thugs.

ALEX: That's just what the commies say.

    Pause.

MARTIN: Oh, no… no…

ALEX: Calm down.

MARTIN: I can't leave the Communist Party. They wouldn't believe me.

ALEX: Yeah, they would.

MARTIN: They wouldn't…

ALEX: You were flicking through *The Little Red Schoolbook* over the weekend. Despite yourself, it got you in. The words struck a chord. You realised the Soviet Union's finished. China. China's the future after all. You ring up Sam Arnold. You—

MARTIN: I can't!

ALEX: Okay. It doesn't matter. Don't worry. You're fine where you are… I think you need a holiday.

MARTIN: I can't leave work.

ALEX: Yes you can. We can arrange it for you. You can have a little accident. We can break your leg.

MARTIN: What?!

ALEX: Not really break it, Marty. We'll send you to one of our doctors and he'll put a cast on for you.

MARTIN: You've got doctors that do that… in Bendigo?

ALEX: Sure we have.

MARTIN: Spy doctors.

ALEX: Yeah.

    MARTIN *smiles a little.*

MARTIN: Who?

ALEX: The Hotham Road Practice… Do you know any of them?

MARTIN: Yeah… Dr Price?

ALEX: No…

MARTIN: Not the woman?

ALEX: No…

MARTIN: Dr Wallace…?

    ALEX *smiles.*

    The old guy. I've been to him. Does he know about me?

ALEX: You know better than that, Martin.

MARTIN: And he'd put a fake cast on my leg.

ALEX: Yeah, just ring up and make an appointment.

> MARTIN *laughs.*

Come up to the city. Meet some of the guys. Take a bit of time off. Have a bit of fun...

MARTIN: I guess.

ALEX: We'll put you up at the Southern Cross.

MARTIN: Yeah?

ALEX: The guys'd love to meet you.

MARTIN: Would they?

ALEX: Shit yeah, the guys in the field, they're the envy of everyone...

> *He suddenly calls out loudly.*

Heh... Heh... Yeah you, number sixteen. Come over here a minute.

> *A* FOOTBALLER *appears. He looks at* ALEX *and then back to the game, checking where the ball is.*

FOOTBALLER: What?

ALEX: Come over here.

FOOTBALLER: What for?

ALEX: I wanna talk to you...

FOOTBALLER: After the game, mate, after the game.

ALEX: No, I wanna talk now.

> *The* FOOTBALLER *stares at him.*

FOOTBALLER: What are you, a talent scout or something?

ALEX: Nah... just want to have a little chat... just in private...

> *The* FOOTBALLER *glances back at the game, and back at* ALEX.

Just a little chat... about the state of the world... There might be something you can do for your country.

VOICE: [*offstage*] Kenny! Kenny!

> *The* FOOTBALLER *looks for who is calling him, then looks back at* ALEX.

FOOTBALLER: Get fucked.

> *He runs off to re-join the game.*

THE END

For a full list of our titles, visit our website:

www.currency.com.au

Currency Press
The performing arts publisher
PO Box 2287
Strawberry Hills NSW 2012
Australia
enquiries@currency.com.au
Tel: (02) 9319 5877
Fax: (02) 9319 3649

www.ingramcontent.com/pod-product-compliance
Lightning Source LLC
Chambersburg PA
CBHW041931090426
42744CB00017B/2009